PDK 21.

GEOGRAPHY

FOR CCEA GCSE LEVEL

Revision Guide

Tim Manson

ISBN: 978-1-78073-063-9

First Edition
First Impression

Layout and design: April Sky Design
Printed by: W&G Baird Ltd, Antrim

Colourpoint Educational
An imprint of Colourpoint Creative Ltd
Colourpoint House
Jubilee Business Park
Jubilee Road
Newtownards
County Down
Northern Ireland
BT23 4YH

Tel: 028 9182 6339
Fax: 028 9182 1900
E-mail: info@colourpoint.co.uk
Web site: www.colourpoint.co.uk

The Author

Tim Manson learned to love Geography from an early age. He is a graduate of QUB, the University of Ulster and the Open University. He has taught GCSE and A Level Geography for over 20 years and now works as Vice Principal at Cullybackey College. He is a Senior Examiner for an awarding body in Geography and is a keen advocate for creative uses of ICT in learning and teaching. He is the author of Colourpoint's popular GCSE Geography textbook, *Geography for CCEA GCSE Level*, which was published in 2013. He has a highly successful website: www.thinkgeography.org.uk

Acknowledgements

Thanks firstly to my family for their support through yet another writing project – especially to my wife Helen and my children, Erin and Isaac. A big thanks to Rachel Irwin at Colourpoint for keeping things moving and keeping me on track, to Wesley Johnston for the diagrams and to Margaret McMullan for making sure that the Geography reflects the current specification. Thanks to my Geography teaching colleagues from my days at Slemish (especially Mike and Gillian) – my first thoughts for this book started with you.

For Helen

Rewarding Learning

Contents

How to use this book ....

This book is designed for use alongside the *Geography for CCEA GCSE Level* textbook as a quick reference guide to the course.

The Revision Material section: revises the key features of the course, the case studies and the key definitions. It also offers revision tips.

These allow you to build up basic definitions of key geographical words throughout the course.

TEST YOUR REVISION

These questions are scattered throughout the text to check how much of the content you have learnt and understood. You can get someone to ask you these questions to test your understanding or test yourself by using a traffic light activity to see if you can answer the question in detail. In a traffic light activity, green means you can answer in detail, amber means you have more revision to do and red means you still have a lot more work to do.

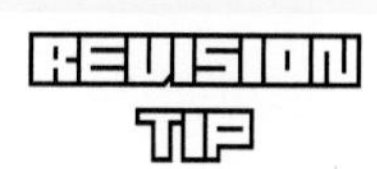

These are scattered throughout the guide to indicate what you need to focus on.

The Practice Questions section: contains some practice examination questions, sample answers and tips on how to answer the questions. It will help you understand the detail that the examiner is looking for in your answers.

Unit 1:
Understanding Our Natural World

1A THE DYNAMIC LANDSCAPE

1. The Drainage Basin
2. River Processes and Features
3. Sustainable Management of Rivers
4. Coastal Processes and Features
5. Sustainable Management of Coasts

PART 1

THE DRAINAGE BASIN

A **drainage basin** is described as the area of land that is drained by a river and its tributaries. When a drop of water falls onto the land (**precipitation**) the force of gravity pulls the water downhill and back towards the sea.

The water cycle

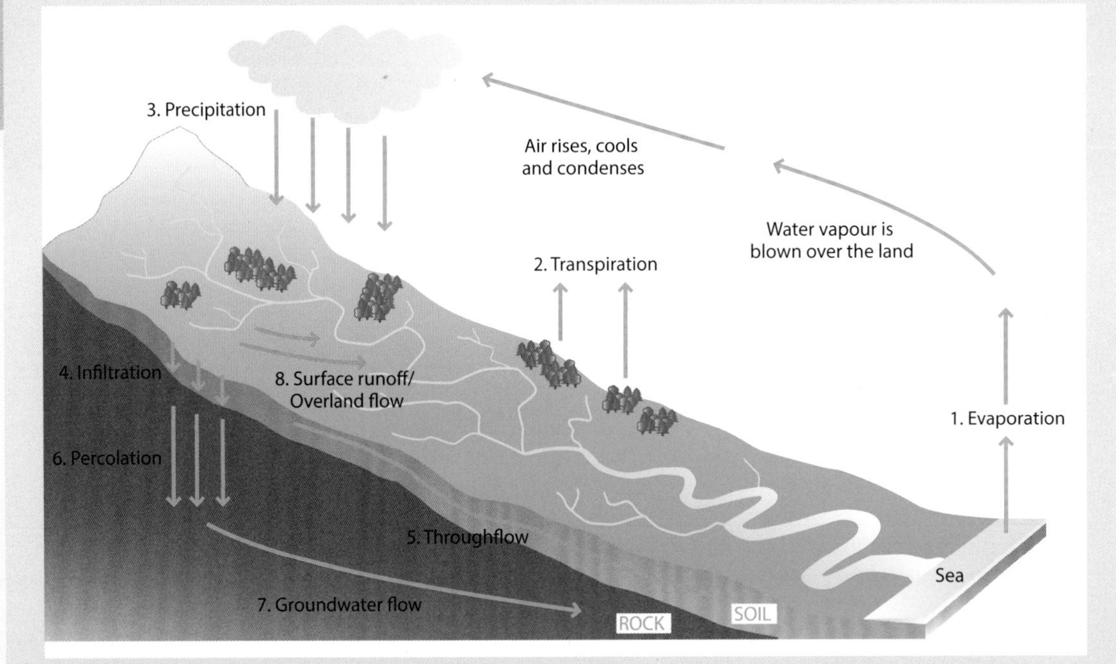

The water cycle

1. Evaporation:
Water is transformed from seawater into water vapour in the atmosphere.

2. Transpiration:
Water vapour is lost from vegetation into the atmosphere.

3. Precipitation:
Water vapour condenses into drizzle, rain, sleet, snow and hail, and this falls towards the surface of the land.

4. Infiltration:
Water soaks (filters) into the soil.

5. Throughflow:
Water moves downhill through the soil.

6. Percolation:
Water moves from the soil into the rock.

7. Groundwater flow:
Water moves slowly through the soil and rock back into the sea.

8. Surface runoff/ Overland flow:
Water moves across the surface of the earth, becoming a stream, tributary or river.

KEY WORDS

Water Cycle: A natural system where water is in constant movement above, on or below the surface of the earth, and is changing state from water vapour (gas), to liquid and into ice (solid).

Watershed: The dividing line between one drainage basin and another.

Source: Where drops of water join to start a river.

Tributary: A small river or stream.

Confluence: Where two rivers meet and join.

Mouth: The place where the river flows into the sea.

The drainage basin system

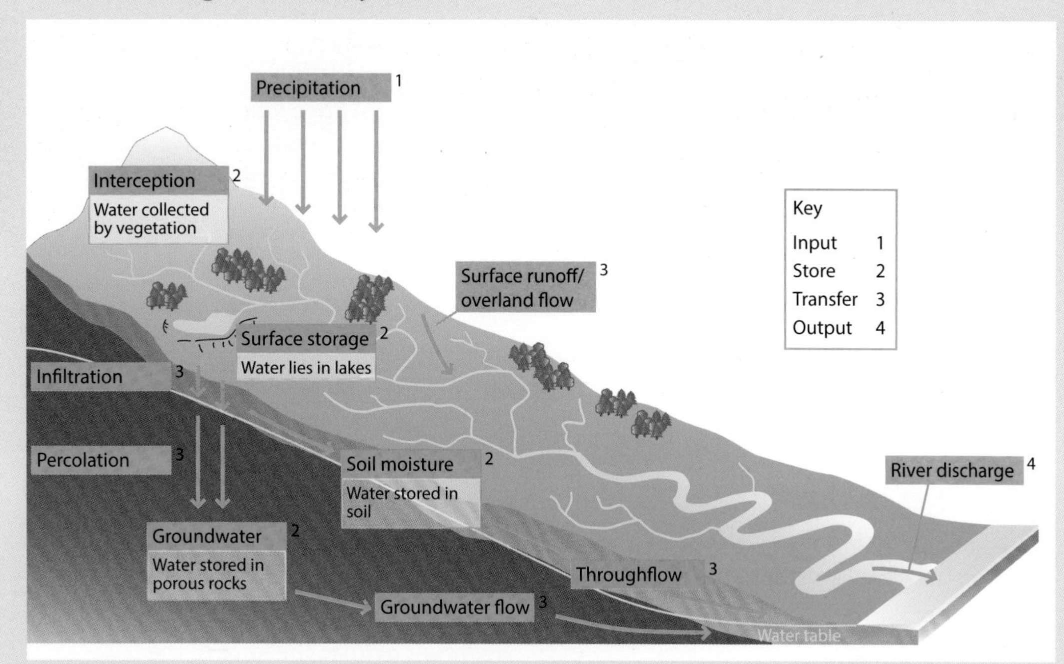

The drainage basin system

1. Inputs: are when water is introduced or put into the system.

2. Stores: occur when water is kept within the system and not moved through it.

3. Transfers: are processes or flows within the system, where water is moved from one place to another.

4. Outputs: occur in the river system when the water is carried through the river and back into the sea.

The characteristics of the drainage basin

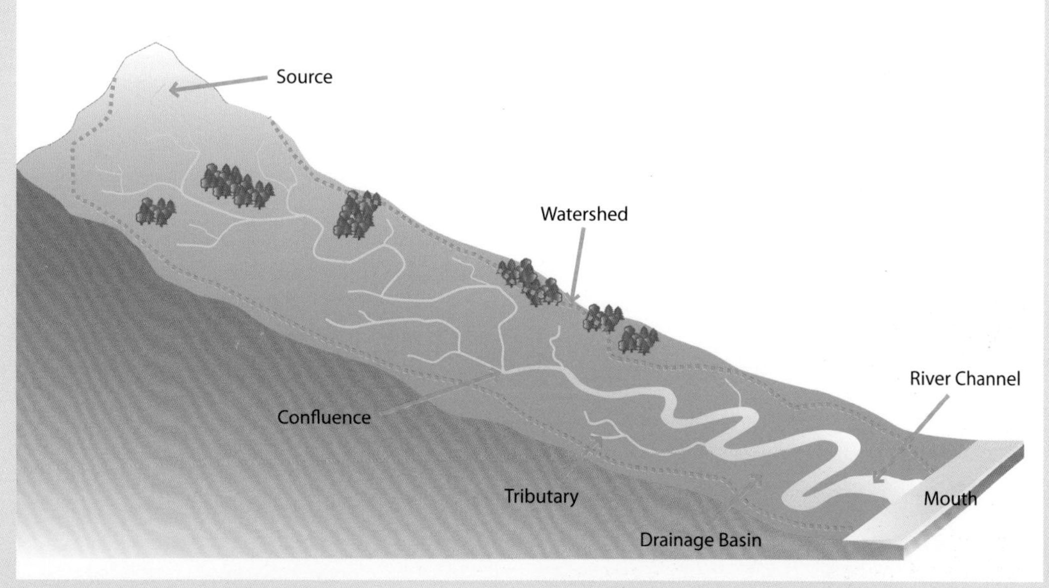

The characteristics of the drainage basin

REVISION TIP

It is really important that you learn the key features of the water cycle and drainage basin system. Learn the definition for each. These are common questions in the exam.

TEST YOUR REVISION

1. Describe the role that evaporation plays in the water cycle.
2. Explain the difference between infiltration and percolation.
3. What is the difference between stores and transfers in the drainage basin system?
4. Draw a diagram of a river and mark the following features: the source, a confluence, the watershed and a tributary.

PART 2 RIVER PROCESSES AND FEATURES

How does a river change along a long profile?

The **gradient** in a river changes throughout the different courses (upper, middle and lower). The upper course is steep but the lower course will be relatively flat. In the upper course, the **depth** and **width** of the river are small but they will both increase as the river continues downhill towards the lower course.

The **discharge** is the amount of water that passes a particular point in a river at a particular time. This is measured as cubic metres of water per second (cumecs).

Cross sectional area (depth and width) m^2	×	Velocity (speed) m/sec	=	Discharge m^3/sec

Processes in the river

Erosion happens in a river when parts of the river bed and/or river bank are worn away and removed from the landscape. The four types of erosion in a river are:

Attrition: When stones carried downstream knock against each other and start to wear each other down.

Hydraulic action: The force of the water pounds into the river bed and banks, and this dislodges more material.

Abrasion/corrasion: The force of moving water throws stones being carried by the river against the river bed and banks, and this dislodges more material.

Solution/corrosion: When weak acid (chemicals) in the water react with the rock and dissolves soluble minerals.

Transportation is when the eroded material is carried from one place to another through the river system. The four types of transportation in the river are:

Traction: This is when the heaviest particles of eroded material are **rolled** along the river bed.

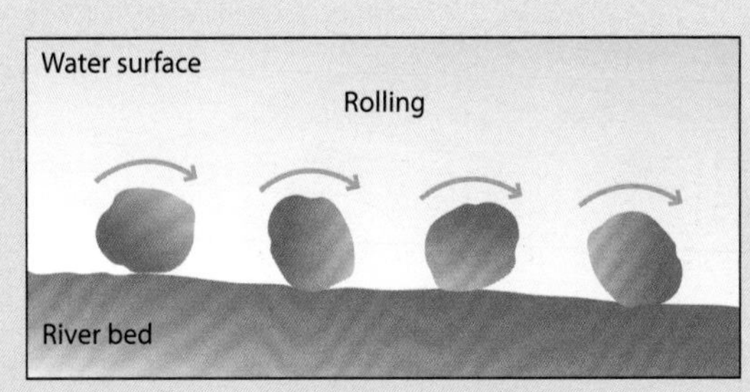

Saltation: This is when some of the heavier particles are not held up in the flow of the river but are **bounced** along the river bed.

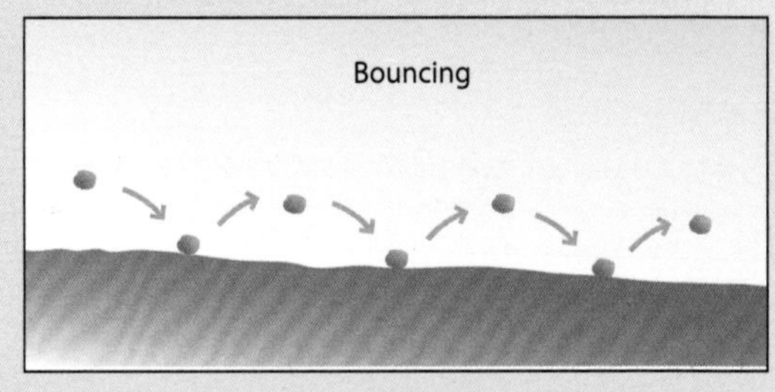

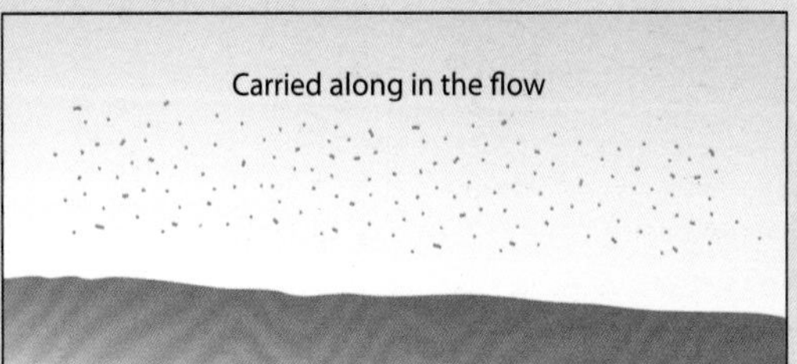

Suspension: As the water speed increases, the river picks up particles. When particles are **carried along in the flow** of the water, they do not make contact with the river bed.

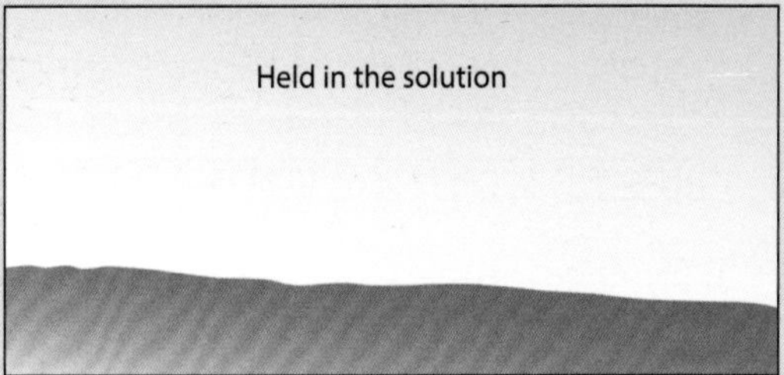

Solution: Some minerals dissolve easily in the water and microscopic particles are **held up in the solution of the water.**

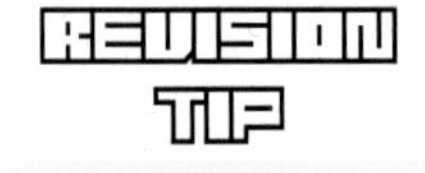

REVISION TIP

It is easy to get confused between the different erosion and transportation processes, so make sure that you learn them carefully. Maybe use the Letter E or T in front of each to remind you which process it is helping to describe.

Deposition is where the river load becomes too heavy for the river to carry and is dumped or deposited along the course of the river.

TEST YOUR REVISION

1. Describe some of the changes you would expect to see in a river from the source to mouth.
2. Why is the gradient of a river different from the upper course to the lower course?
3. How would you calculate the discharge of a river?
4. Describe the difference between erosion and transportation.
5. Explain how abrasion helps to erode the river banks.
6. Describe the conditions that cause traction to take place in a river.

Changes in the river characteristics and the load downstream

As the river moves from the upper course, through the middle course to the lower course, some of these river characteristics should change:

- The shape of the river channel increases downstream (the river should get wider and deeper).
- The velocity of the river increases downstream.
- The discharge increases downstream.
- The river bedload becomes more rounded and smaller further downstream.

It is the erosion, transportation and deposition processes which change the shape and characteristics of the river. Erosion is the main factor, increasing river depth and causing faster flowing water towards the outside of the meanders. This causes more hydraulic action and the formation of river cliffs. Deposition may also be evident on the inside of river bends, where water travels slowly and deposition beaches are built up over long periods of time.

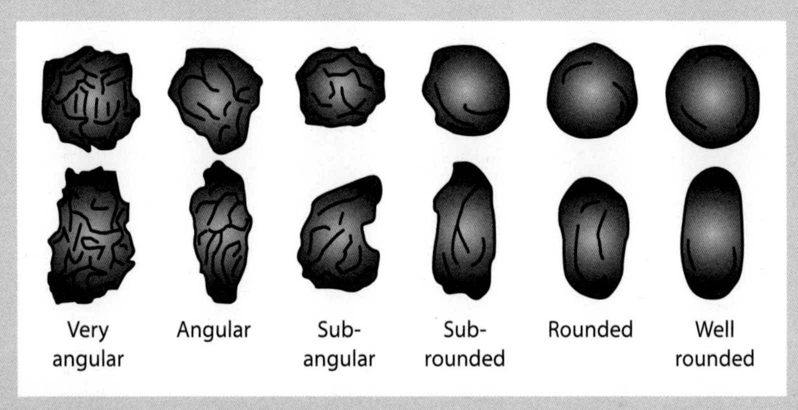

The Power's Scale of roundness (used to observe the degree of stone angularity/roundness)

The size and shape of bedload changes dramatically through the course of a river. The stones are angular in the upper course but the sharp edges become worn down as they journey towards the lower course.

REVISION TIP

A common exam question shows some bedload data from a river fieldwork event and asks you to describe and explain the processes that have been working on the river. You will need to be aware of the river changes downstream and the different ways that erosion, transportation and deposition work on the river.

River landforms

Waterfalls occur when rivers move from an area of hard rock to an area of softer rock. Hydraulic action, abrasion and attrition all work to erode the softer rock, which is transported and deposited further downstream. Often the edge of the waterfall recedes, creating a gorge.

The formation of a waterfall

Hard igneous rock (basalt)

Soft sedimentary rock (limestone)

The river increases in speed here because there is no friction

Erosion

Soft rock is easily eroded to create an overhang

Force of water (hydraulic action) erodes a plunge pool

Overhang extends to reveal a ledge of hard rock

Hard rock becomes too heavy for the soft rock and cracks begin to form

Hard rock breaks off and the waterfall recedes (moves backwards)

Eroded material is transported through the river system

REVISION TIP

Make sure that you can explain the changing features of how a waterfall erodes in detail and are able to support this by drawing a diagram.

Meanders occur as water moves downstream and the increased speed (velocity) of the water allows erosion to take place.

Cross section through a meander

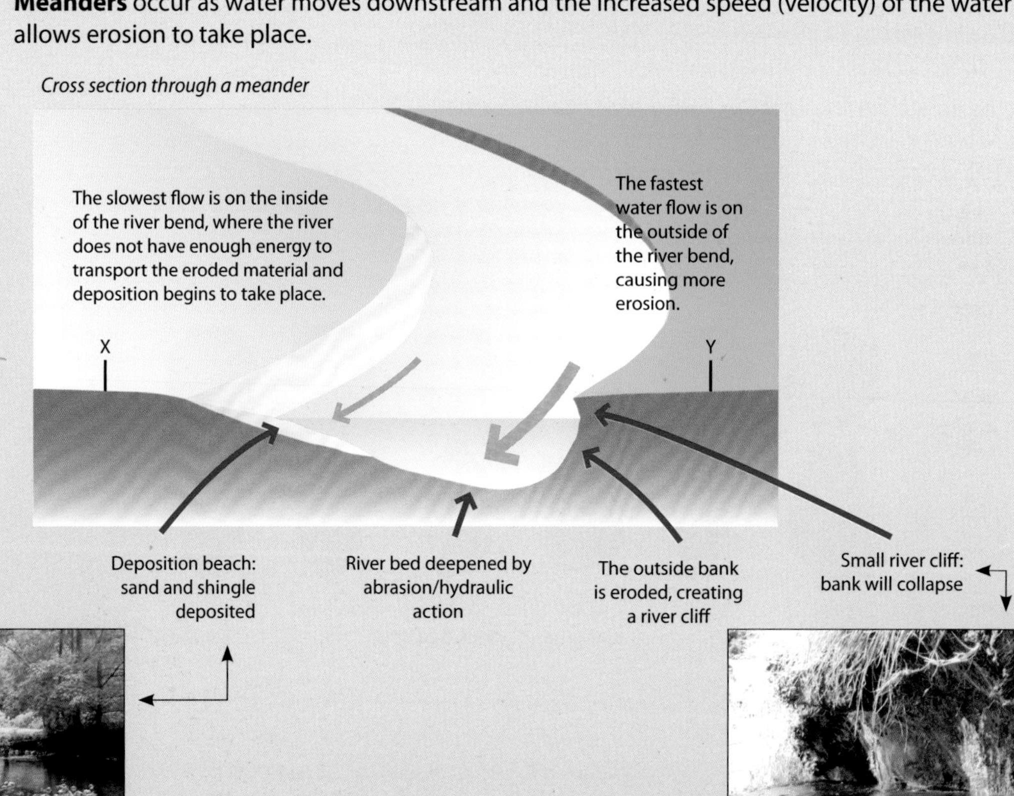

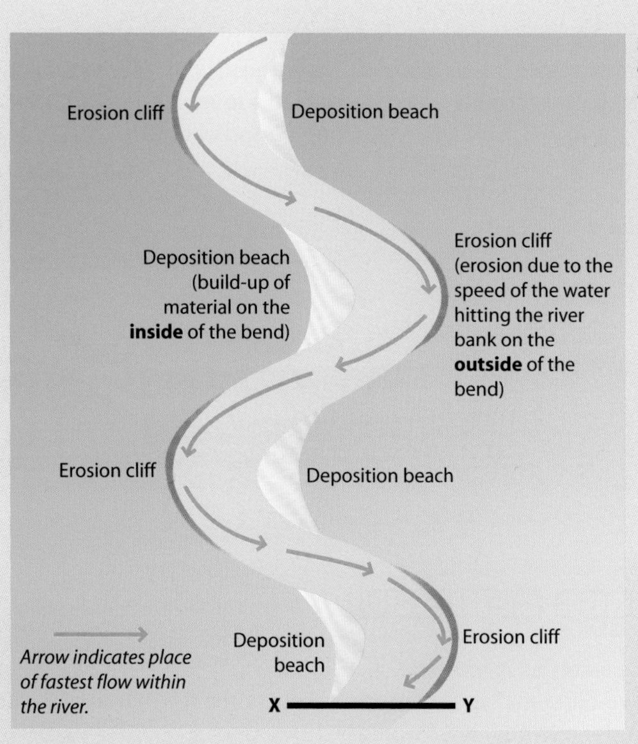

Erosion and deposition in the river channel

In many river systems the transition from middle to lower course is often marked through the development of **ox bow lakes.**

The formation process of ox bow lakes

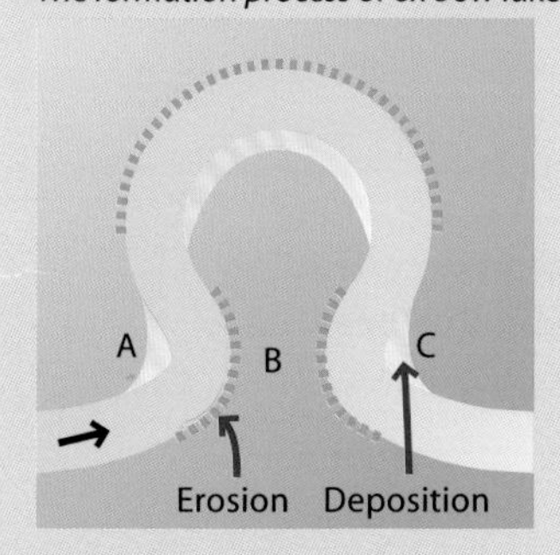

Step 1:
The river is meandering as usual, with deposition taking place on the inside of the bend (A and C) and erosion occurring on the outside of the bend to create river cliffs (B).

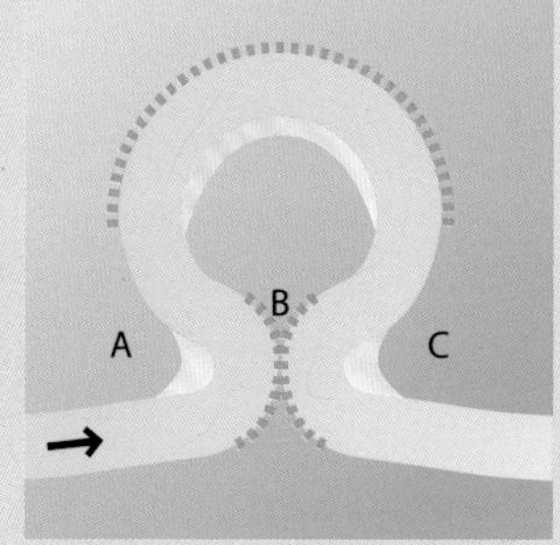

Step 2:
Erosion continues at B, on the outside of the bend. During a river flood, when the velocity and discharge of the river are much higher, there is more erosion and the river cuts through the neck.

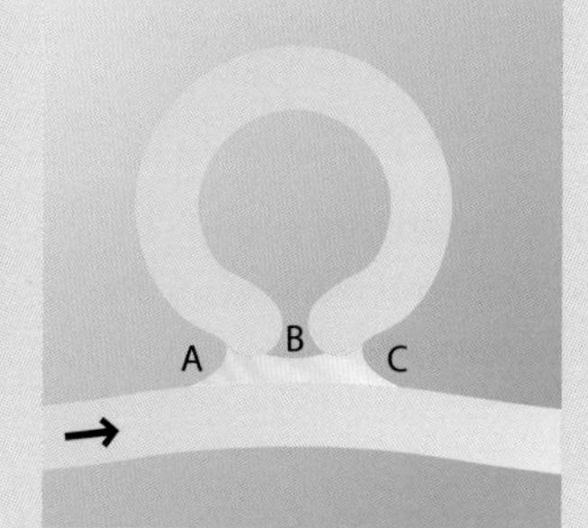

Step 3:
Deposition takes place and starts to block up the neck of the river (A, B and C). The meander is permanently cut off from the new, straight river channel.

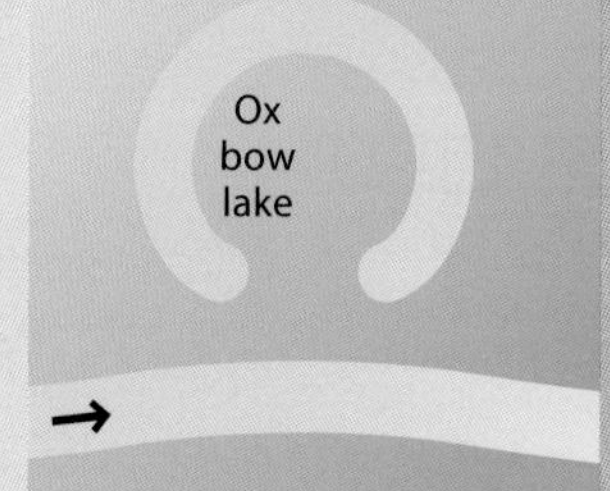

Step 4:
The former river channel now forms an 'ox bow lake', where the water will gradually infiltrate into the soil and evaporate, leaving the river bed exposed and likely to be populated by surrounding plant species over time.

Floodplains are areas of land that have been covered with the silt deposited by the changing course of the river. It is the area of land over which the river is likely and able to flood.

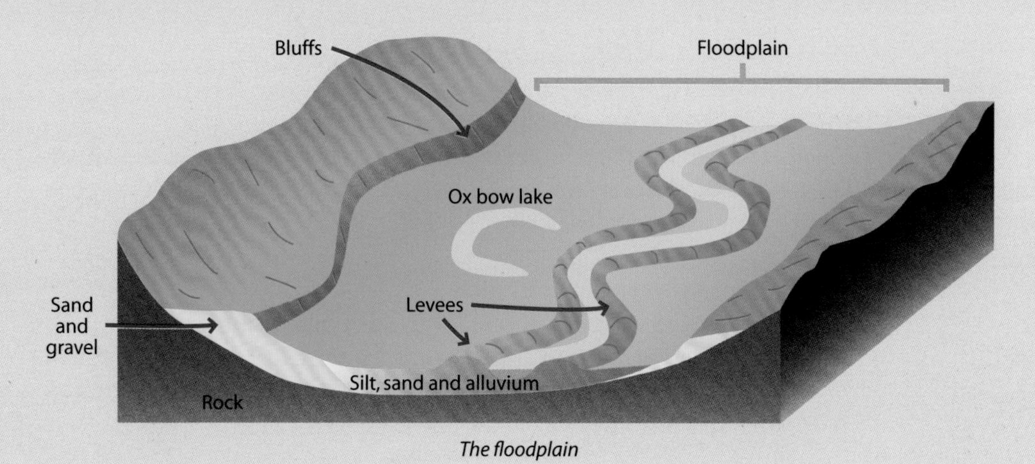

The floodplain

The main role of rivers is to transport material and this often causes flooding. As the river floods, it will deposit material across the valley floor. The largest, coarsest material will be deposited first, close to the riverbank. This forms a raised bed called a **levee.** Levees are formed by the repeated flooding of the river and will build up over a long period of time.

Exam questions often test how well you know the details of how each river landform is formed. Make sure you that you can explain the different erosion, transportation or deposition processes that work to create each landform.

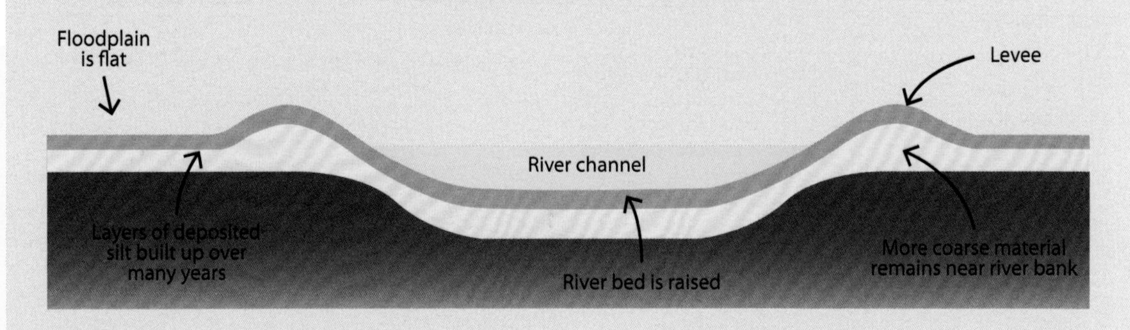

TEST YOUR REVISION

1. Describe how a waterfall is formed.
2. Explain how two different types of erosion work in the formation of a waterfall.
3. What is a meander and how is it formed?
4. What is a river cliff and how is it formed?
5. Describe and explain the processes that form an ox bow lake.

Land use near rivers

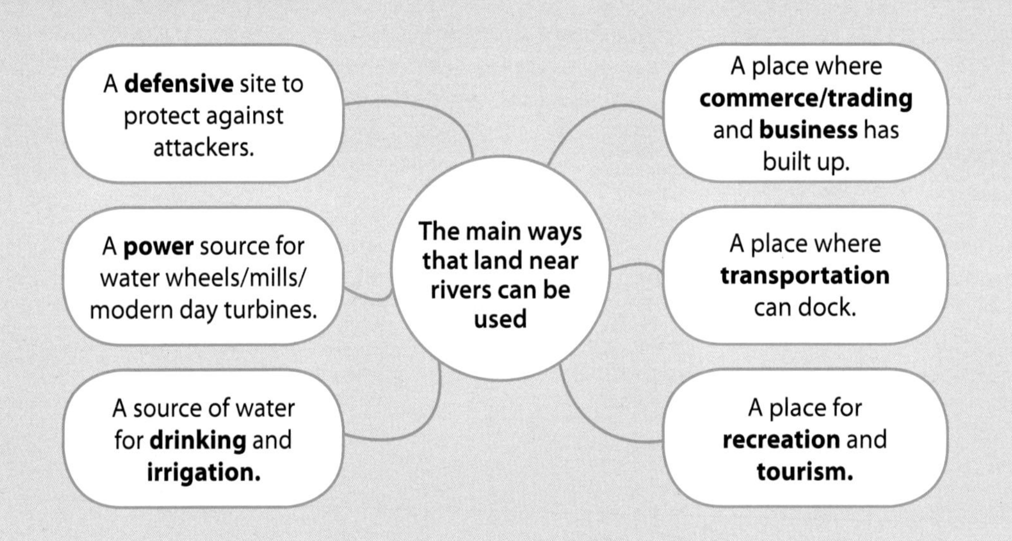

REVISION TIP

Photos and maps can often be used in examinations to help you to apply your knowledge and understanding of rivers and coasts. Use some of the practice questions later in this book to help you to work out how this works.

BASIC MAP SKILLS REVISION

Scale and distances

Scale takes real life things and reduces them in size many times so that they can be shown on a map. The OS maps used in the GCSE exams will be at a scale of 1:50,000. This means that 1 cm represents 50,000 cm or 1 cm = 500 m (or half a kilometre).

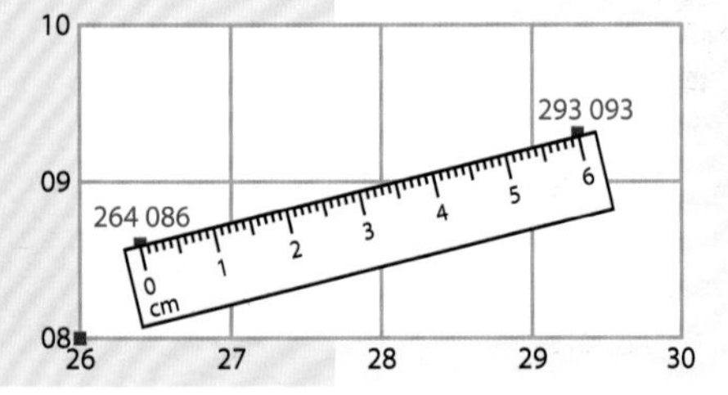

- ***Measuring a straight line distance***

The easiest way to work out distance is to use a ruler to measure from one point to another on the map and then use the scale to work out the distance in kilometres. In the example opposite, the distance has been measured as 6 cm, which is equivalent to 3 km of real distance.

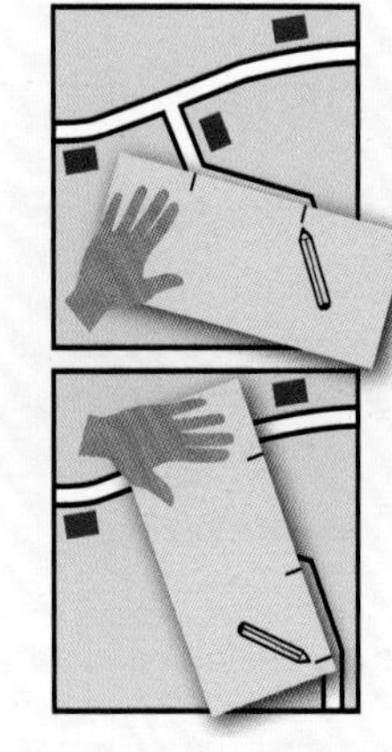

- ***Measuring a route (non-straight line) distance***

In an exam, the best way to measure a route or non-straight line distance is to use the edge of a piece of scrap paper.

1. Place the corner and straight edge on your starting point.
2. Then pivot the paper until the edge follows the route you want to take.
3. Every time the route changes direction, make a small mark on the edge and pivot the paper so that the paper follows the route again.
4. Repeat this process until you complete your route.

Four figure grid references

OS maps are covered in a series of blue grid lines. These grid lines help you to pinpoint an exact location on the map through the use of a unique number called a grid reference.

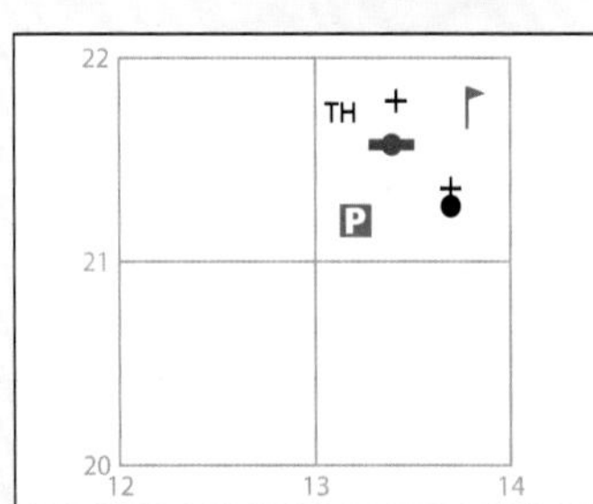

A four figure grid reference will help you to identify the location of a square on the map. Read the number along the bottom (or top) of the map before you read the number up the side. In the example opposite, all of the symbols are found in square 1321.

Six figure grid references

A six figure grid reference will help you to identify the precise location of a point within a square on the map. The first two numbers indicate the square that the point is found along the corridor (the bottom or top). The fourth and fifth numbers indicate the square that the point is found up the stairs (the side). The third and sixth numbers are gained by drawing an imaginary grid on top of the square and assigning a number from 0 to 9 across the square.

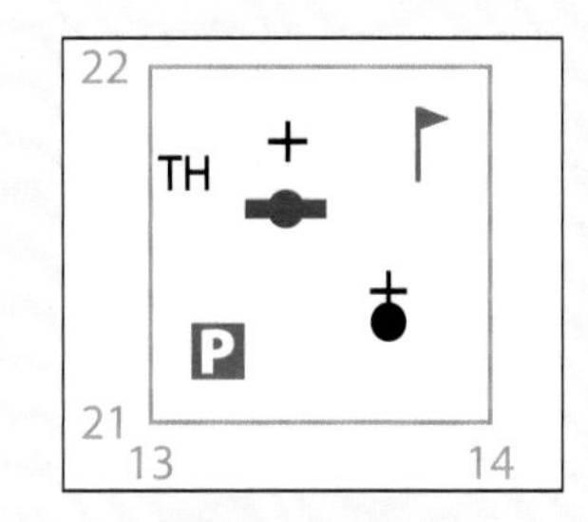

In the example opposite, all of the symbols have a four figure grid reference of 1321 but only one symbol has the precise location of 132 212. Which one? It might help to draw the grid shown but you won't have time to do this during an exam, so you will have to practice this skill. What are the precise six figure grid references for the other symbols in this square?

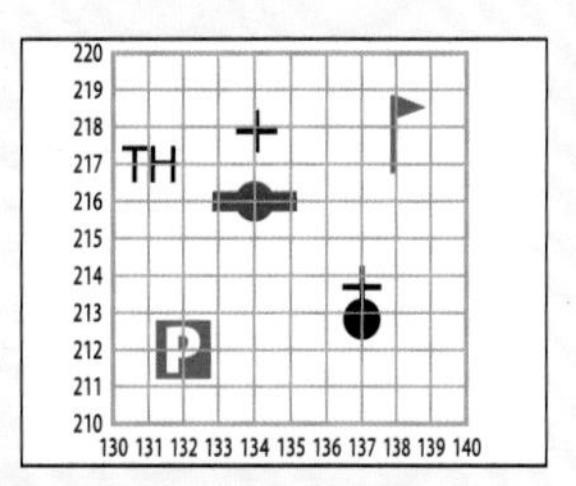

Using symbols

Symbols are used on maps to represent important features so that the map does not become too cluttered. The good news is that any map you get in an exam will have the key attached, so you do not need to learn the symbols. However, during your rivers and coasts revision, it is a good idea to look specifically at the water features and tourist information (shown below), as these are the main things that you will have to look for.

Water Features				Tourist Information		
Cliff	Lightship Beacon	Highest point to which tides flow		Information Centre	Golf Course	Youth Hostel
Flat Rock	Lighthouse in use : disused	Marsh or salting		Parking	Camping Site	Place of interest
High Water Mark (mud and shingle, sand)	Lake : Lough : Pond	Ferry (V)	Ferry (vehicle)	Picnic Area	Caravan Site	Public Telephone
Low Water Mark	Footbridge; Canal : Canal (dry)	Ferry (P)	Ferry (passenger)	Viewpoint	Bus Station	Waymarked Walks

Relief on maps

Relief is the shape and height of the land. There are three different ways that heights can be shown on an OS map.

- ***Spot heights:*** A spot height is shown on a map as a black dot with the height of the land written (in metres) beside it.
- ***Contour lines:*** These are brown lines that are drawn onto maps which show the height of the land above sea level. A contour is a line that joins places with the same height. On 1:50,000 maps the contour line will go up every 10 m. The closer together the contour lines are, the steeper the land will be. The further away the lines are, the gentler the slopes will be.
- ***Colour-shaded areas:*** Some maps also use different colours within the contours to indicate the height of an area. The darker the colour, the higher up the place is located.

REVISION TIP

Basic Map Skills

The GCSE Geography specification states that you should have the opportunity to:

- read plans and maps to be able to use number coordinates and both four and six figure grid references.
- explore the ways in which relief is represented on OS maps (1:50,000), identify major relief features and relate cross sectional drawings to relief features.
- measure straight and curved line distances.

(Adapted from CCEA GCSE Specification in Geography, © CCEA 2015)

PART 3 SUSTAINABLE MANAGEMENT OF RIVERS

The causes of flooding (physical and human)

Floods happen when there is a temporary, extra amount of water in the river system, which causes the amount of water in the river channel to overflow, covering areas of land and the surrounding flood plains that are usually dry.

Physical causes

- **Precipitation:** The more water that falls onto a drainage basin over a short period of time, the quicker the water will be forced to become surface run-off.
- **Land use/vegetation:** Vegetation tends to intercept water and slow the passage of water into the river system.
- **Soil and underlying rock:** Sandy soils allow rainwater to infiltrate quickly, whereas clay soils stop water passing through and can increase surface run-off at a faster rate. Some rocks are permeable (porous) and allow water to pass through (eg limestone) whereas other rocks are impermeable (non-porous) and water is unable to pass through them (eg slate).
- **Steepness of drainage basin:** If the slopes of the land are steep in a drainage basin, water will be drained quickly and can lead to a flash flood.

Human causes

- **Deforestation:** If trees are removed this will increase the amount of surface run-off into the river channel and the risk of flooding.
- **River management:** Narrowing the river channel or building a bridge in an inappropriate position can reduce the river capacity.
- **Urban growth:** Urban areas generally have good drainage systems that move any excess water into the river channel quickly.
- **Global warming:** Increased melting of ice stores due to processes associated with global warming could lead to more water than usual in the drainage basin systems.

Case Study: Causes of the Boscastle flood, 2004 (a case study from the British Isles)

Date: 16 August 2004
Location: Boscastle (Cornwall, England)
Rivers involved: Valency, Paradise and Jordan

Causes of the flooding

Physical factors

Prolonged rainfall	• It rained 12 days out of 14 days in August.
Heavy rainfall	• A large depression (low pressure) produced thunderstorms. • On 16 August, 200 mm of rainfall was recorded over 24 hours. • Most of the rain fell in a five hour period.
Steep valley sides	• The valley sides are very steep throughout the area. • The river rises to more than 300 m in 6 km. • The water flows very quickly through the river system.

Human factors

Deforestation	• This meant there was little interception and water moved into the river channel quickly.
Urbanisation	• The old Victorian sewage system could not cope with the excess water.
The bridge factor	• Some of the bridges over the River Valency and River Jordan were old, small arches that quickly got blocked with flood debris and felled trees. The blockage acted like a dam and caused a surge of water when it was released.

REVISION TIP

It is really important that you learn some key facts and figures to support your case study answers. For this study, you should know at least two physical and two human causes of flooding in detail.

The impacts of flooding

ON PEOPLE		
• Causes damage to property (eg water damage). • Causes crops and animals to be lost.	• Hits poor people hard (especially in LEDCs) as many have no insurance to help rebuild after a flood. Aid may be needed.	• Causes public health issues (eg water mixing with sewage can lead to problems with drinking water and increase waterborne diseases).
ON THE ENVIRONMENT		
• Brings excess water, which will replenish drinking water supplies and help with irrigation (eg the River Nile).	• Brings alluvium (silt) to allow crops to grow in desert areas. • Allows fish to breed and to swim upstream to their breeding grounds.	• Washes chemicals, waste and sewage into rivers, causing pollution and killing wildlife and vegetation.

TEST YOUR REVISION

1. Describe two causes of flooding in relation to your case study for a river in the British Isles.
2. Explain the impact that flooding had on people and the environment.

River management strategies

Hard engineering strategies require major changes to the river (eg building new walls) to try and prevent it from flooding. These measures are not sustainable in the long term.

Soft engineering strategies require limited changes to the river (eg afforestation) to manage rather than prevent flooding.

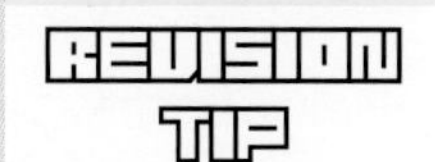

TIP

Make sure that you have a clear understanding of the difference between a hard and soft engineering strategy.

Hard engineering strategies

1. Channel enlargement (deepening and widening)	+ Increasing the size of the river channel allows it to carry more water. + Water is moved more efficiently during flood events. - The channel needs regular work as silt can build up on the river bed. - The heavy machinery needed can be expensive and can harm delicate ecosystems.
2. River straightening	+ Rivers that meander are sometimes straightened to help increase the velocity. + Property developers prefer straight river banks for building complexes and farmers prefer regular field shapes. - Sometimes rivers will try to revert to their original channel. - Fish like to lay their eggs in the shallow parts of river bends.

Dams: A dam is a wall that stops the river from moving downstream, controlling the amount of water that can travel through the river system.

Levees: A levee is usually created when a river floods and deposits material on the flood plain close to the river banks.

Embankments: An embankment is an artificial flood wall which can be built on either side of the river.

Flood walls: A flood wall is built from a material designed to increase the depth of the river channel. It prevents water from reaching the flood plain, even if the river floods above the riverbank.

Washlands: This area of land acts as a storage area, where river water can 'wash' into during a flood. It is usually found in the lower course of a river.

3. Levees and embankments (flood walls)	+ Levees and embankment walls can be built along the river banks to allow more water through the river channel before the water reaches flood level. - These can be expensive. - If water does break through an embankment it can be more destructive because the water will travel faster. - The natural process of silting on the flood plain will be prevented by levees and embankments.
4. Dams/ reservoirs	+ A dam controls the risk of flooding. + It can produce HEP which is a cheap and renewable method of energy production. + Man made lakes and reservoirs can be used for recreation. - Both are extremely expensive. - Both have a major impact on the natural environment, changing the ecosystem completely.
5. Storage areas	+ Water can be pumped into temporary lakes (storage areas), which will reduce the amount of flow in the river. - It takes up a lot of space.

Soft engineering strategies

1. Land use zoning	+ Land within a floodplain is divided up into areas which experience different degrees of flood risk: • Red zone = places with a high chance of flooding (non-residential land, parks, farmland). • Amber zone = flooding is possible but unlikely (car parks, sports facilities). • Green zone = flooding very unlikely (residential housing). - Does not prevent flooding.
2. Afforestation	+ Planting trees in the upper course of a drainage basin will help reduce floods as trees intercept and store water. +/- Does not prevent flooding but can help reduce its likelihood.
3. Washlands	+ Land can be farmed and only used in flood emergencies. + Can help increase friction and slow the river down. - Can be difficult to find available land close to cities.

Sustainability

The exam may ask you to consider the sustainability of these different engineering measures.

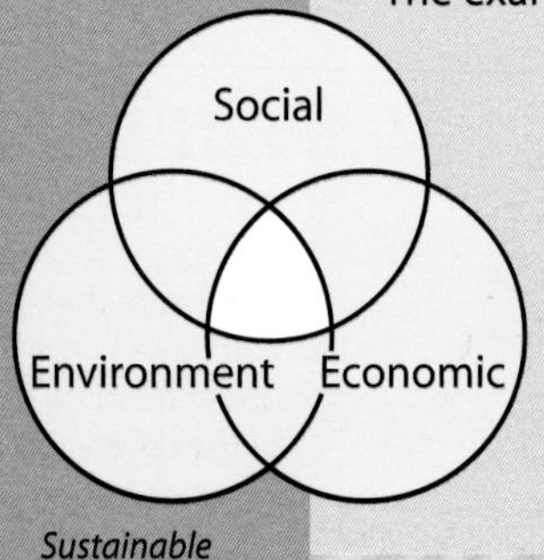

Sustainable development

Social sustainability: Is the strategy something which will add to people's lives? Will it allow them to live close to each other without risk of death or injury?

Economic sustainability: Is the strategy expensive to build and maintain or is it just a one off cost? Will the strategy last for a long time?

Environmental sustainability: Is the strategy good or damaging to the environment? Does it help protect wildlife and animal habitats?

TEST YOUR REVISION

1. What is the difference between hard and soft engineering strategies?
2. Name and describe three hard engineering strategies.
3. Name and describe three soft engineering strategies.
4. Choose two engineering strategies and evaluate how sustainable they are.

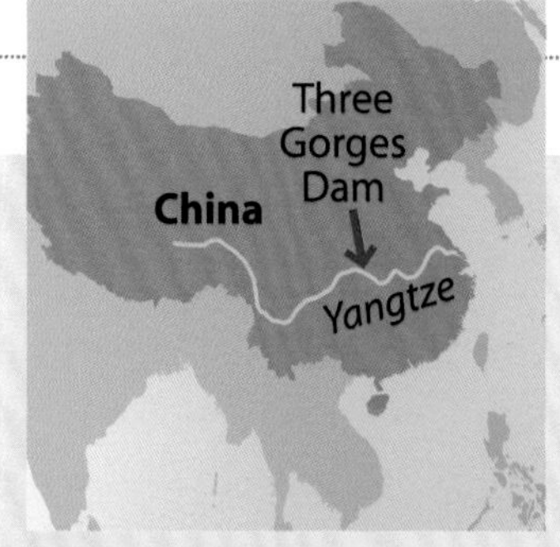

Yangtze river location

Case Study: The Yangtze river, China (a case study from outside the British Isles)

CASE STUDY

Location: Yangtze (Changjiang) river, China

The need for a river management scheme

Due to the population explosion in China from the 1950s onwards, the amount of human activity around the Yangtze river has increased the impacts of any flood event.

River management strategies used

Strategy	Description	Advantages	Disadvantages
1. Three Gorges Dam Project (TGP) (Hard)	• The TGP controls a drainage area of 1 million km². • The TGP can provide flood storage for 22.15 billion m³ of water. • The TGP built a 185 m high dam across the Yangtze. Work started in 1994 and cost £50 billion. • The lake area is 1,000 km². • The building of the dam flooded 140 towns and forced the evacuation of 1.2 million people.	• The dam is designed to protect 100 million people downstream. • The dam will regulate the amount of water in the river. • The dam produces 'green' HEP energy.	• Most floods in recent years happen below the TGP. • There are often earthquakes and landslides in the area. • Much of the land used for resettlement has poor soils and is unsuitable for farming. • With more people now living in urban areas, concentrating the population, this has increased the amount of pollution and sewage in the area. • The dam has devastated local ecosystems. • The river dolphin (Baiji) is close to extinction.
2. Levees (hard)	• Over 3,600 km of levees have been built along the river channel.	• These levees have been built to protect 80 million people. • They are designed to handle a 10 to 30 year frequency flood.	• These levees are not always effective. In 1998 the Yangtze flooded over the top of the levees, killing 3,000 people and leaving 30 million homeless.
3. Washlands/ detention basins (soft)	• These are low lying areas/ lakes that are set aside for temporary flood storage. • There are 40 major basins which can store 50 billion m³ of water.	• They are easier to construct than dams. • Land can be used for other purposes such as farming.	• The Dongting lake has become silted up and this can increase flooding risk. • The area is unsafe during flooding. There is no flood proofing for buildings or main roads to ensure swift evacuation. • In 1998 300,000 people had to be moved to safety.
4. Flood warning systems (soft)	• Sensors placed in the upper course of the river will give warning of increased/dangerous water levels.	• These might give people time to move out of an area. • 180 monitoring stations have been built on the Yangtze.	• The system cost over £9 million.

REVISION TIP

The command word 'Evaluate' is often used in questions that require specific case study knowledge.

Remember that an evaluation should look at both the advantages and disadvantages of a strategy.

In this study, you need to discuss the good and bad points of two different management strategies.

It might be easier to look at one hard and one soft or one more sustainable and one less sustainable strategy.

Examiners will be looking for solid detail in any answer and a concluding statement explaining which strategy is best.

How sustainable are these projects?

The government would argue that these methods of river management are sustainable, particularly the dam as it:

- has saved lives.
- produces clean electricity.
- allows safe transport through the river systems.
- means that there is a consistent water supply during droughts.

Others would argue that all of the management strategies are not sustainable as they:

- damage the environment (eg caused landslides, brought the river dolphin close to extinction).
- cost far too much.
- flooded the homes of millions of people and caused their relocation.
- risk catastrophe if the dam ever bursts its banks.

TEST YOUR REVISION

Evaluate two river management strategies used on a river that you have studied outside of the British Isles.

PART

PART 4: COASTAL PROCESSES AND FEATURES

Constructive and destructive waves

Waves are created by the transfer of energy as the wind blows across the surface of the sea. The size of any wave depends on its **fetch**. The fetch is the distance that a wave travels in open water. The longer the fetch, the larger the potential wave is likely to be.

As waves begin to approach the shore, the water which rushes up the beach is called **swash** and the return flow is called **backwash**.

Fetch of waves

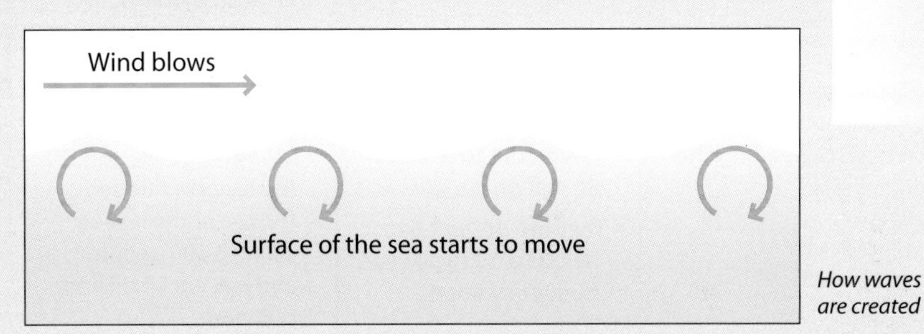

How waves are created

Constructive and destructive waves

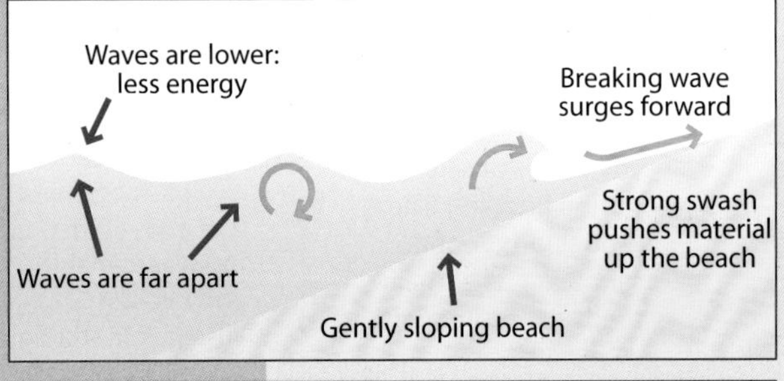

Constructive waves

These help to build up a beach. They are gentle, flat and low (around 1 m in height), and their energy is limited with only a few waves per minute (between six and nine).

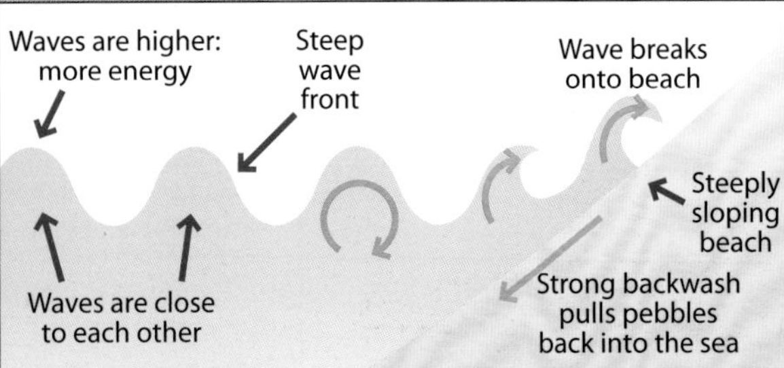

Destructive waves

These help to erode a beach. They have a lot of energy, they are steep (up to 3–4 m high) and close together, and they have more waves per minute (around 15 per minute) than constructive waves. Their strong backwash pulls material back into the sea to create a steep beach.

What are the processes found at the coast?

1. Erosion

Corrasion/abrasion: The force of the moving water in the sea throws the stones that it is carrying against the coastline and cliffs, which dislodges more material.

Attrition: Stones and boulders that are being carried by the sea knock against each other and start to wear each other down. This knocks the edges off the stones and results in smaller and rounder stones.

Solution/corrosion: Salts and acids in the seawater slowly dissolve coastal cliffs.

Hydraulic action: The force of the water pounds into the cliffs and dislodges more material.

2. Transportation

Material in the sea is transported using the same four methods as rivers (traction, saltation, suspension and solution) but most material is carried along the coast in a process called longshore drift.

3. Deposition

Eroded material is transported along the coastline and is deposited to form a beach.

Waves usually approach the coast from the same direction as the wind.
Backwash returns material back down the beach at 45 degrees to the swash.
Wooden groynes slow down movement along the beach
Material is moved along the coastline in a zigzag course.
Wind direction
Direction of longshore drift
Build up of sand

Longshore drift transporting material along the coast

What coastal landforms are found at the coast?

1. Erosional landforms

Bays and headlands: are formed when outcrops of harder, resistant rock and softer, less resistant rock are found in the same areas. Waves gradually erode the softer rock away, leaving the harder, more resistant rock sticking out into the sea.

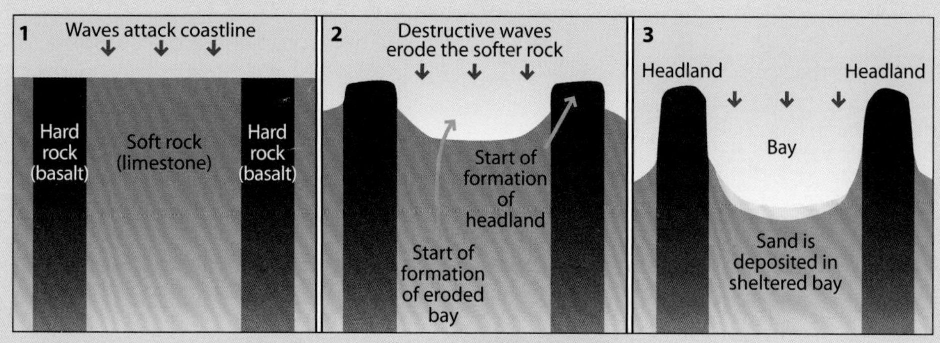

The formation of bays and headlands

A wave cut notch: is formed as waves start to undercut the foot of a cliff. The notch continues to widen and undermines the foundation of the cliff face, which causes the cliff to collapse and retreat backwards.

A wave cut platform: gets left behind as the cliff retreats further away from the original position. These are gently sloping flat platforms that can be seen at low tide.

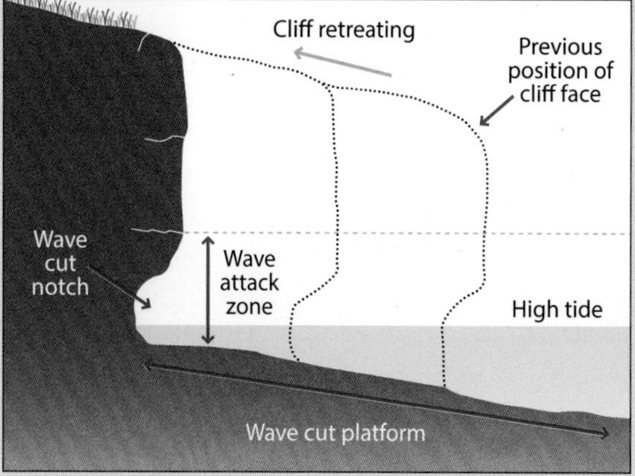

Wave cut notch and platform

Cliff: A high, steep rock face that is caused by coastal erosion.

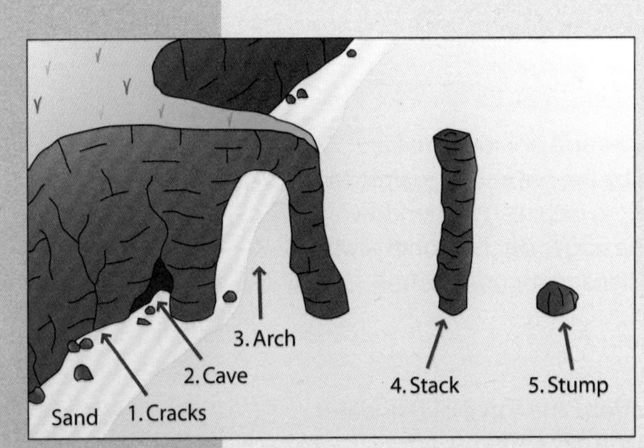

Cliffs, caves, arches and stacks

Erosion processes will continue to attack the rocks in a cliff over time.

- The **cracks** in the rock will face erosion through hydraulic action and attrition, and the continuous impact of the water will widen any weaknesses in the rock and split the crack into a cave.
- If the **cave** is being formed in a headland, the cave might continue to be eroded to form an **arch**.
- Waves will continue to erode (especially at the base of the foot of the arch) until the weight of the rock becomes too heavy and the roof of the arch will collapse.
- This exposes a **stack**, which will continue to come under attack from waves. It will eventually be undercut and will be worn away to leave a **stump**.

2. Depositional landforms

A beach: is a gently sloping area of land that is found between the high and low water tide marks. They are built up by constructive waves moving beach and deposited material (sand, shingle and pebbles) up the beach.

A spit: is a long, narrow ridge of land that is made up from deposited material (sand and shingle) along a coastline.

A hooked spit: is a deposition feature, which includes a narrow ridge of land that is hooked in shape and usually occurs where there is a change of direction along the coastline.

The formation of a spit

There are a number of conditions needed before a hooked spit can form:

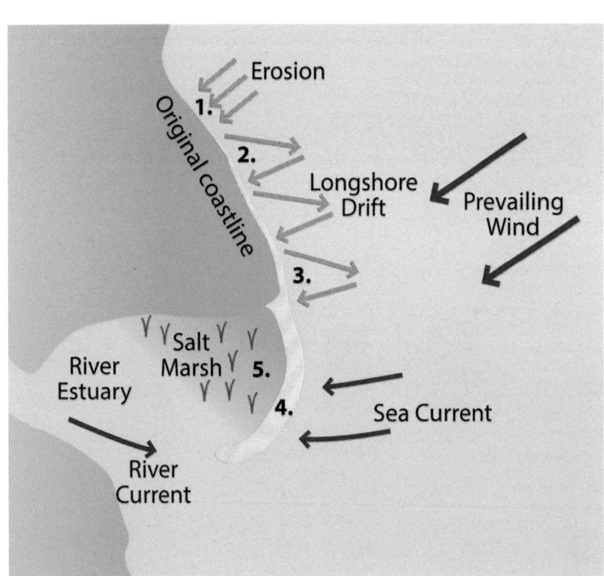

The formation of a spit

- They are found in areas where the material forming the coastline is easily eroded. **(1)**
- They are formed when prevailing winds help to transport material down the coast using longshore drift. **(2 and 3)**
- They occur where the coastline changes direction (usually where a river estuary meets the sea).
- The energy from the sea and the river meet at one place and this is where deposition takes place. **(4)**
- Often the area behind the spit will become a salt marsh. **(5)**

REVISION TIP

Make sure that you learn the different coastal processes and features in detail. Examiners often ask you to explain how features are formed. These questions are worth high marks.

TEST YOUR REVISION

1. Describe the two different types of wave found at the coast.
2. Explain how bays and headlands are formed.
3. Explain the processes which have taken place to create a stump along the coastline.
4. Describe how a hooked spit is formed.

PART 5: SUSTAINABLE MANAGEMENT OF COASTS

Why does human activity in the coastal zone often lead to conflict?

The coast has become a highly desirable place for people to live and work for a number of reasons:

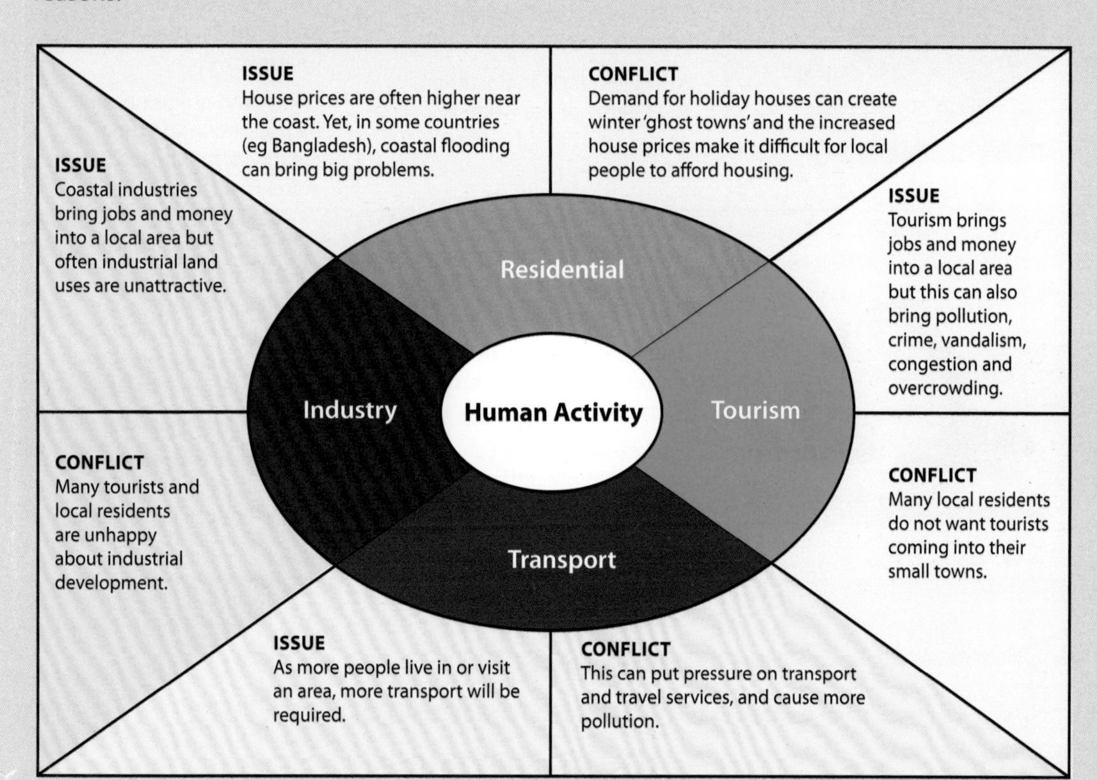

The need for coastal defences

With so much money now invested in business, industry and housing at the coast there is a greater need to protect the coast from erosion. Strategies include:

Strategy	Description	Evaluation
1. Keeping the sea out		
Sea Walls	• Hard engineering method usually made of concrete. • They support the land and hold back the sea. • Wave action beats against the sea walls without eroding the coast. • They are built to absorb and deflect wave energy.	• Can be expensive. • They need deep foundations so they do not erode away. • They can be ugly. • They might not solve the erosion problem but just move it elsewhere.
2. Retaining cliffs and beaches		
Groynes	• These are wooden, concrete or rock barriers than can be built out into the sea. • They trap the sand carried by longshore drift to help build up a deposition beach. • They are usually considered a hard engineering method.	• They can trap sediment that is supposed to go somewhere else. This moves the erosion problem to another place. • They are very cost effective. • They need continual maintenance and repair.

Strategy	Description	Evaluation
Gabions	• These are metal cages that are filled with rocks. • They are stacked together to create a wall of rock. • As waves crash against them, the energy of the water is absorbed inside the cage.	• They are cheap. • They can be a good short term solution. • They break apart easily and some see them as unattractive. • Debris and pollution can be trapped inside them creating a habitat for animals such as rats.
Beach nourishment  Source: U.S. Army Corps of Engineers photo by Ann Cameron Siegal	• This is when sand or pebbles are added to a beach – replenishing it or building it up. • Usually a soft engineering method if the sand is brought from a sustainable source. • A large, wide beach can naturally protect the coastline as wave energy is absorbed through the sand.	• This method can have the least environmental consequences and works well in combination with other measures (such as groynes). • This can be very expensive and will require constant maintenance and protection.

REVISION TIP

Make sure that you know the difference between coastal management strategies that keep the sea out and those that are used to retain cliffs and beaches.

CASE STUDY

Location: Newcastle, Co Down, Northern Ireland

Case Study: Newcastle, Co Down (a coastal management strategy from the British Isles)

The new seafront promenade in Newcastle, built in 2007

Why did the coast need to be managed?

- Sand from the 8 km long beach was being lost due to longshore drift, leaving the beach with shingle and stones, and no sand to attract tourists.
- Shops, houses and businesses were damaged in a flood in 2002.
- The sea wall was damaged in storms (most recently in 2002).
- Key tourist attractions (eg Royal County Down golf course) needed to be protected.

Coastal management strategies used

Strategy	Description	Positive impacts	Negative impacts
Groynes	Groynes were initially built to protect the beach in the 1950s. More were built in the 1980s to collect the beach material as it was moved along the coast.	Stops sand being removed from the beach and builds the beach up, making the area attractive to tourists.	Groynes erode and break apart over time and can be expensive to replace. They can be unattractive and often make access to the beach difficult.
Gabions	In the 1990s, further measures were needed to protect some of the sand dunes along the coast. The gabions were ineffective and had to be replaced about 10 years later.	A good, inexpensive, short term solution to stop erosion.	Not a long term solution as cages split under pressure from the sea. Can be unattractive, and build up debris and pollution.
Rock armour	Large rocks were used to protect the coastline from erosion.	A good, cheap solution to stop erosion.	Can provide a breeding ground for rats and other animals.
Sea wall	In 2007, over £4 million was spent redesigning the seafront. The beach had been badly eroded and a new curved sea wall was built to help protect the main street from waves and floods.	Can be used to provide protection and also to make walkways for tourists. Will protect businesses and houses from floods and large waves.	A very expensive solution that can have a big impact on the natural environment, completely changing the features of a place. It often just shifts erosion further along the coast.

Evaluation of the coastal management techniques

- The new promenade development has won many design awards and local residents hope that this will help to rejuvenate the tourism industry.
- Concerns were raised by environmentalists about how the 'hard engineering' has completely changed the face of the coastline with minimal benefit.
- Some argue that this new construction is ugly, has damaged the natural environment (and animal habitats) and has replaced natural sand dune, which is much better for beach protection.

TEST YOUR REVISION

1. Describe why tourism and transport can both create conflict in the coastal zone.
2. Describe how sea walls work and evaluate their sustainability.
3. Why did the coast at Newcastle need to be managed?
4. Identify and describe which coastal management strategy you think is the most sustainable for Newcastle.

REVISION TIP

If an exam question asks you to refer to **one** coastal management strategy you should refer only to one of the measures used to protect the coast but make sure that you can clearly explain how and why it works.

1B OUR CHANGING WEATHER AND CLIMATE

1. Measuring the Elements of the Weather
2. Weather Systems Affecting the British Isles
3. The Causes and Consequences of Climate Change

PART 1

MEASURING THE ELEMENTS OF THE WEATHER

The difference between weather and climate

Weather is the day-to-day state of the atmosphere (the layer of gases that surrounds our planet). It is a dynamic process which is constantly changing.

Climate is more long term. It is the average weather taken over a long period of time (usually over 35 years). Climate is a less dynamic process and does not change as quickly as the weather.

Measuring the elements of the weather

Element	Description of element	Method of measurement	Unit	Description of equipment
Temperature	A measure of the amount of heat in the atmosphere.	Max and Min thermometer (instrument)	Degrees centigrade (°C)	Max and Min thermometer records the range of temperature from the highest and lowest daily temperature.
Precipitation	The amount of moisture in the atmosphere, involving water in all of its states: liquid, solid and gas (vapour). This includes water, dew, hail, rain, sleet and snow.	Rain gauge (instrument)	Millimetres (mm)	Precipitation (usually as rain) is collected in a rain gauge.
Wind direction	The air in motion in a horizontal direction.	Wind vane (instrument)	8 compass points	The direction from which the wind is coming from can help to tell us important details about what type of weather we can expect.
Wind speed	This speed can change from calm to hurricane force.	Anemometer (instrument)	Knots per hour (kph)	An anemometer is a device which helps to measure the speed of the air.
Air pressure	The pressure exerted by the weight of the atmosphere on the earth's surface. The normal pressure is set at 1000 mb. Low pressure is anything below this and high pressure is above this.	Barometer (instrument)	Millibars (mb)	If pressure is rising or falling this will help indicate how the weather is likely to change. An aneroid barometer can be used to measure pressure.
Cloud cover	The cover (or amount) is reported as eighths (or oktas) of the sky covered.	Observation	Oktas (eighths)	An observer will estimate the amount of blue sky that is visible and identify how much of the sky is covered in cloud.
Cloud types	A cloud is a visible mass of tiny particles floating in the atmosphere, consisting of water formed from the condensation of water vapour.	Observation	Stratus Cumulus Nimbus Cumulonimbus Cirrus	Clouds are found at one of three layers in the sky: low, middle or high.

REVISION TIP

Make sure that you know the details of how to measure/observe the seven weather elements in detail and be sure to understand some of the factors that need to be considered when locating weather instruments – accurate readings are very important.

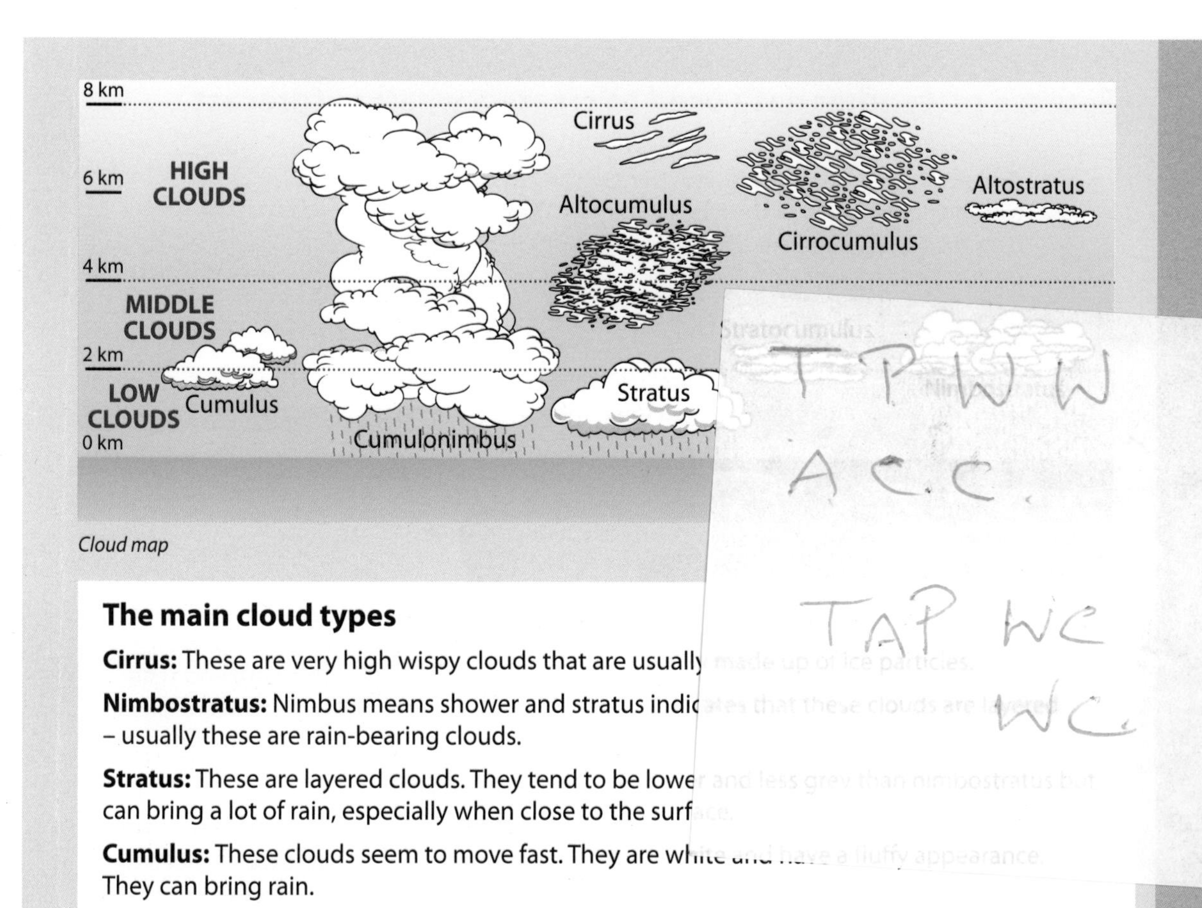

Cloud map

The main cloud types

Cirrus: These are very high wispy clouds that are usually made up of ice particles.

Nimbostratus: Nimbus means shower and stratus indicates that these clouds are layered – usually these are rain-bearing clouds.

Stratus: These are layered clouds. They tend to be lower and less grey than nimbostratus but can bring a lot of rain, especially when close to the surface.

Cumulus: These clouds seem to move fast. They are white and have a fluffy appearance. They can bring rain.

Cumulonimbus: These are cumulus clouds that gather moisture. They start to tower as air rises and can trigger hail, thunder and lightning.

Factors to consider when locating weather instruments

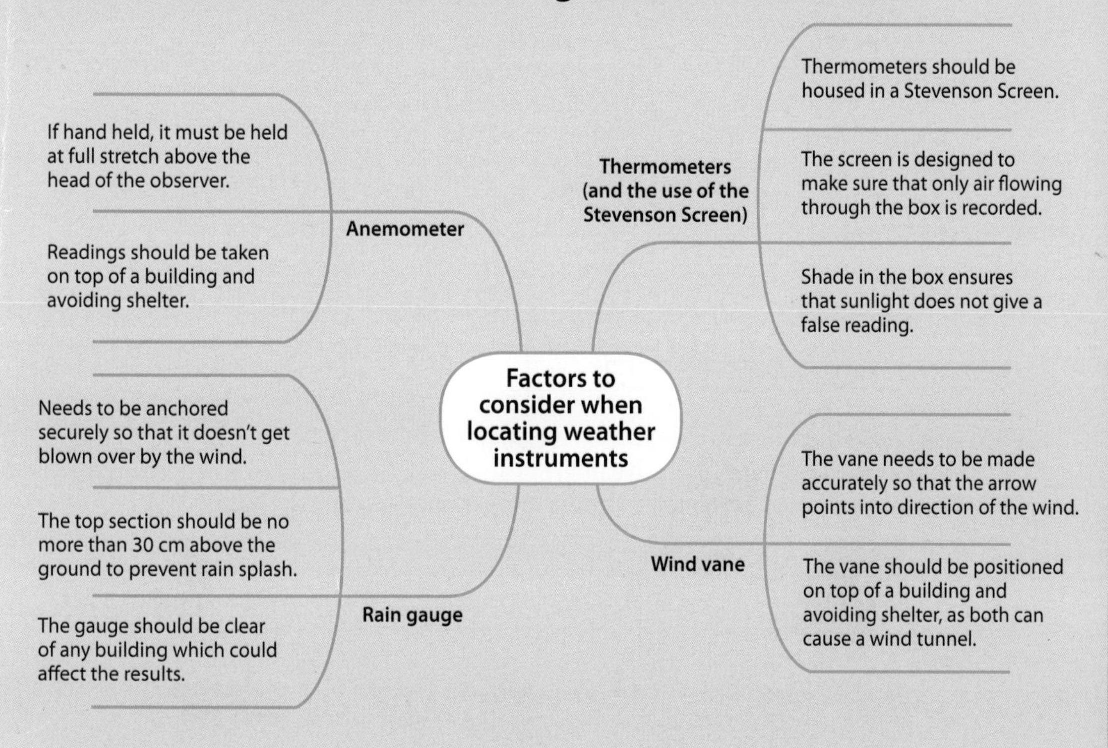

Sources of weather data used to create a weather forecast

Geostationary satellites hover over the same spot on the earth, moving at the speed of the earth's rotation. They usually remain over the equator and are generally at an altitude of 36,000 km, eg European Meteosat.

Polar-orbiting satellites pass around the earth from pole to pole at a height of 850 km. They pass the same point on the earth every 12 hours. The satellite will provide pictures of the clouds and information about the temperature, eg the US NOAA satellites.

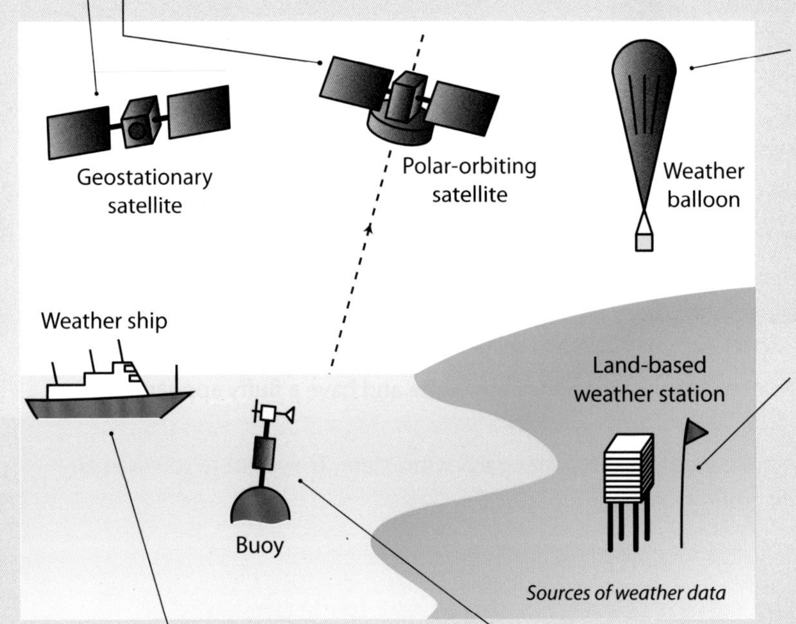

Sources of weather data

Balloons: A rubber balloon is filled with helium and a recording package (radiosonde) is used to record and send information back to earth from the upper atmosphere.

Land-based weather stations: 30 weather observation stations in the UK help to take weather measurements and observations every hour.

Weather ships: Most ships carry weather recording equipment. In the past weather ships were used to collect weather information, eg *MS Polarfront*.

Buoys: Moored and floating (drifting) buoys are used to record and send weather information back to weather centres.

TEST YOUR REVISION

1. What is the difference between weather and climate?
2. What are the seven elements of the weather?
3. Describe how you would accurately measure temperature and precipitation in the atmosphere.
4. Explain some of the factors that need to be considered when positioning a rain gauge.
5. Describe the main sources of weather data that could be used to create a weather forecast.
6. What is the difference between a geostationary and a polar-orbiting satellite?

WEATHER SYSTEMS AFFECTING THE BRITISH ISLES

PART 2

The temperature and moisture characteristics of the air masses affecting the British Isles and their seasonal variation

What is an air mass?

An **air mass** is a large parcel of air (often thousands of kilometres wide) which stays still over a place for a long period of time, picking up the area's temperature and moisture characteristics.

Polar maritime (Pm)

- This is the most common air mass affecting the British Isles.
- It originates over the north Atlantic Ocean.
- It reaches the UK from the west or north west.
- It produces unstable air that creates cumulus and cumulonimbus clouds but has good visibility between showers.
- It can also cause convectional rainfall in the summer months.

Tropical maritime (Tm)

- This is a very common air mass over the British Isles.
- Its air travels from the warm southern Atlantic Ocean and moves over the south west of the British Isles.
- It brings mild conditions in the winter and warm but wet weather in the summer.
- It is responsible for bringing dull skies (nimbostratus clouds), drizzle and fog (poor visibility).

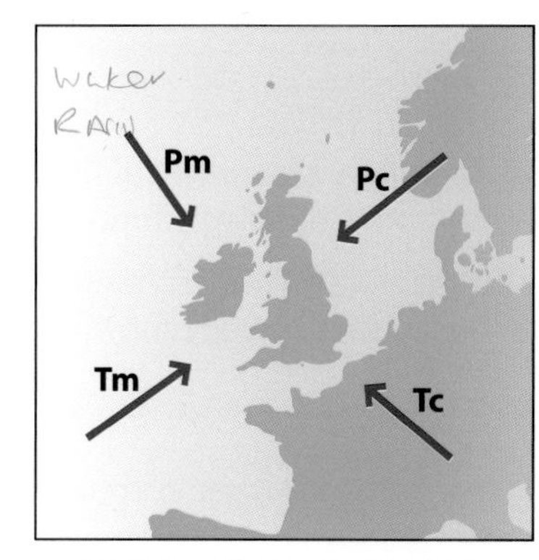

Air Masses affecting the British Isles

Polar continental (Pc)

- This is more prevalent in the winter than the summer.
- Its air originates over Northern Europe (Norway/Sweden) and moves from the east/north east.
- It produces very cold conditions in the winter but milder conditions in the summer.
- Its air can be unstable in the winter and can bring snow showers along the east coast of England.
- It usually brings dry but cool conditions (with Stratus cloud).

Tropical continental (Tc)

- This is the least common air mass affecting the British Isles and usually only in the summer.
- Its air travels from North Africa and the Mediterranean.
- It brings very warm and dry air from the south and south east.
- It brings mild conditions in the winter but hot weather (heat wave) in the summer.
- It can cause thunderstorms to develop if the temperatures rise.

Questions that relate to the different characteristics brought by air masses appear often in exams, so make sure that you know the difference between the four main air masses.

The weather patterns associated with depressions and anticyclones as they move across the British Isles

Across the British Isles there are two separate weather systems that control our weather:

1. **Depression**
   A low pressure system usually associated with unsettled weather and bands of wind, rain and even snow in winter.
2. **Anticyclone**
   A high pressure system usually associated with settled weather and cloudless skies.

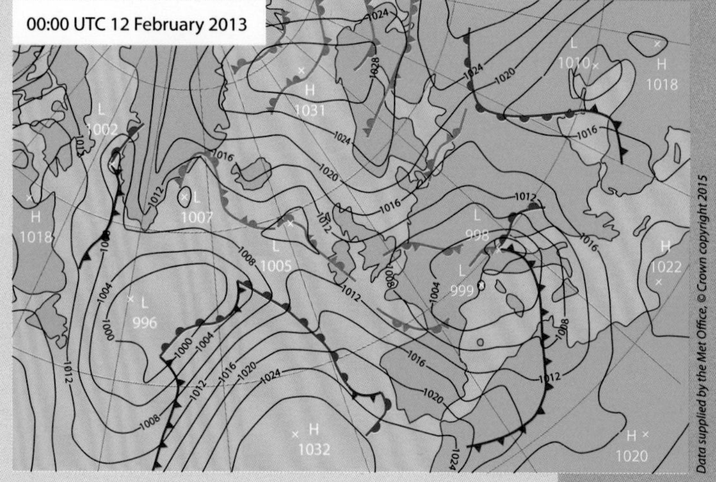

A Met Office surface pressure chart for 12 February 2013

The influence of pressure and wind

Surface pressure charts are often used to record atmospheric pressure. Isobars are the black lines used to join places with the same atmospheric pressure. When isobars are close together this indicates increased pressure and strong winds. When isobars are spaced apart the wind tends to be gentle.

How weather fronts are formed

1. A cold front: This is a moving block of cold air, bringing a change in weather and a narrow belt of rain and clouds.

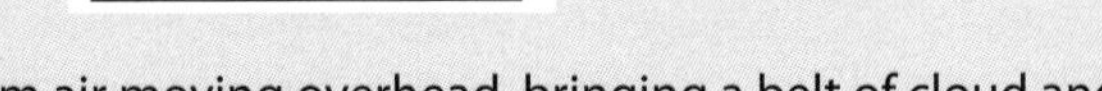

2. A warm front: This is a block of warm air moving overhead, bringing a belt of cloud and some rain. The rain will gradually increase as the front gets closer.

3. An occluded front: This is where warm air has started to rise up over cold air. The weather here will be the same as at a cold front but without much cloud or rain.

KEY WORDS

Front: The leading edge of a mass of air which has a different temperature and different characteristics from the air beside it.

Weather charts

A synoptic chart is a weather map that gives a snapshot of the weather across a region, summarising a large amount of complicated, detailed information.

A plotted surface chart is a chart containing all the information that is generated from surface weather observations or from automated sites (usually shown as triangles rather than circles).

Weather observation

The weather taken at a particular weather centre/station could look like this:

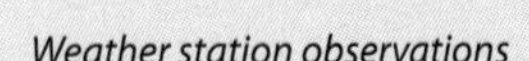

Weather station observations

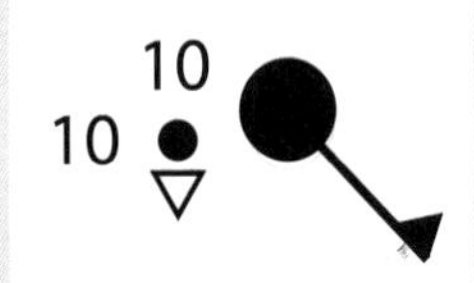

This can be explained in the following way:

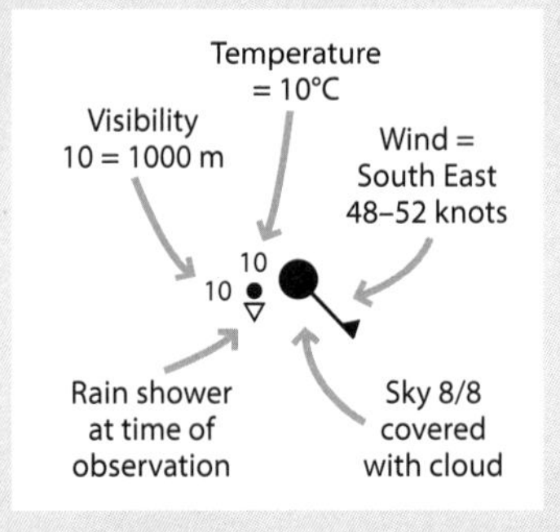

The symbols are explained below:

Cloud cover

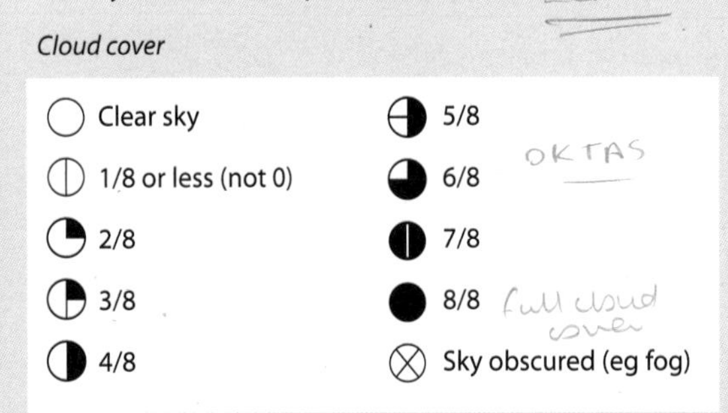

The circle that indicates the weather centre also helps to show the observed cloud cover.

Precipitation

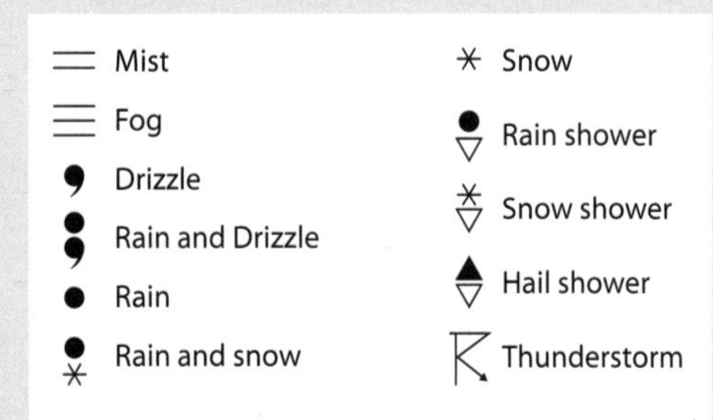

The type of precipitation that is currently falling is usually shown underneath the temperature measurement.

Wind speed

Symbol	Speed	Symbol	Speed
◎	Calm		28–32
	1–2		33–37
	3–7		38–42
	8–12		43–47
	13–17		48–52
	18–22		53–57
	23–27		57–62 etc

The wind speed is usually recorded as a 'shaft', which also points to the direction where the wind is coming from. The 'feathers' on the end of the shaft help to indicate the speed of the wind.

TEST YOUR REVISION

1. What is an air mass?
2. What are the main differences between the four main air masses?
3. Describe the weather you would expect if a tropical maritime air mass was the most dominant.
4. How can you tell wind speed on a surface pressure chart/synoptic chart using isobars?
5. What is an occluded front?

Depressions across the British Isles

Depressions are areas of low atmospheric pressure which produce cloudy, rainy and windy weather.

The formation of a depression

In the UK, a depression is formed out in the Atlantic Ocean when cold, polar maritime air from the north moves south and meets some warm, tropical maritime air moving up from the south. The lighter, warm air will start to rise up over the denser, cold air and will develop into a front.

The passage of a depression

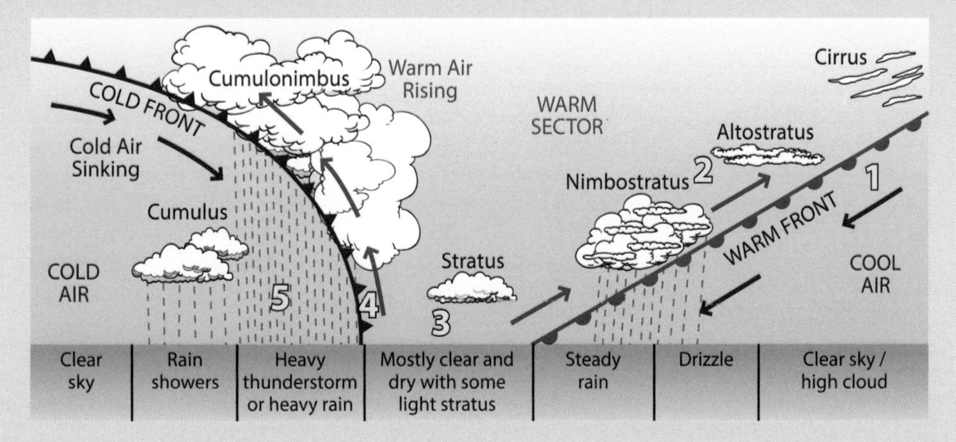

Weather will change as a depression passes overhead.

1. At the warm front, the lighter, warmer air from the south (tropical maritime) meets colder air from the north (polar maritime) and it starts to rise.
2. Warm air rises over the colder air and as the air rises, it cools, the water condenses and clouds start to form (altostratus and nimbostratus). This results in steady rain.
3. As the warm sector passes, the warm air slowly rises, cools and condenses over the centre of the low pressure system. Weather can be settled but this does not last long.
4. As cold front moves in, the colder, heavier air from the cold front meets the warmer air. The cold air starts to undercut the warm air and forces the warm air higher into the atmosphere. Fast moving air can produce high winds and cool temperatures.
5. As warm air is forced to rise, clouds will be formed (cumulonimbus and then cumulus clouds). The result can be heavy thunderstorms and heavy rain showers that will clear as the front continues.

Anticyclones in the British Isles during the summer and winter

Anticyclones are areas of high pressure, which are usually bigger than depressions and produce calm, settled weather with little cloud cover or precipitation.

The formation of an anticyclone

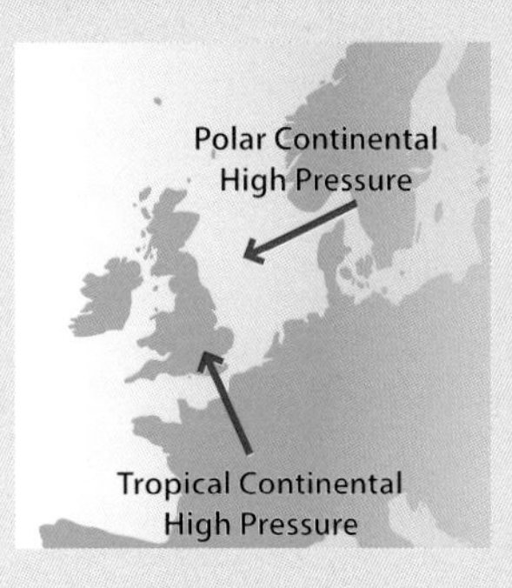

The high pressure system which creates an anticyclone comes from the south of the UK. Tropical continental air masses bring warm and dry weather north into the British Isles.

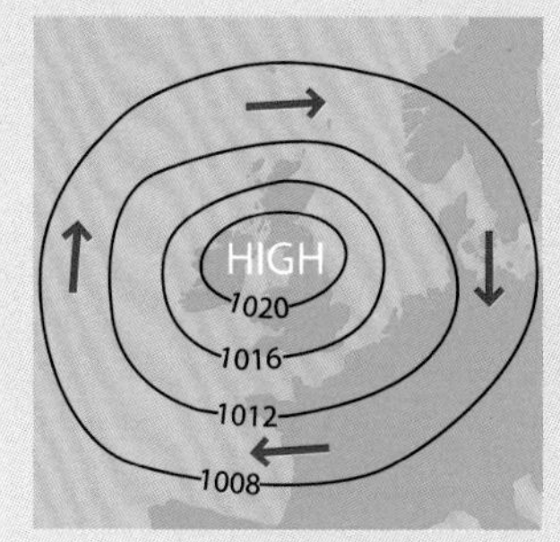

The air sinks from high altitude and as it descends, it absorbs any moisture and stops condensation from taking place. Anticyclones are large, powerful weather systems that can stay in place for long periods of time and will 'block' other weather systems from moving in.

Key features of depressions and anticyclones

The formation and features of an anticyclone are largely the same in summer and winter but the impact can be a bit different.

Features	Depressions	Summer anticyclone	Winter anticyclone
Pressure	Low pressure and falling (below 1000 mb).	High and increasing (over 1000 mb).	High and increasing (over 1000 mb).
Temperature	Temperature will vary depending on the type of air that is passing overhead.	In the summer the temperatures can be warm, as air is coming from the warm south. The hot, sunny days (when there is a lack of clouds) allows the air temperature to be high (around 24°C on average).	In the winter temperatures are much lower than during the summer, as the sun is low in the sky, reducing the heat received.
Cloud cover	A wide and varied selection of clouds can be found as a depression passes.	Sinking air means there are settled conditions with few clouds and clear skies. Lack of cloud cover allows daily temperatures to be increased. At night, clear skies mean that heat will escape back into the atmosphere and overnight temperatures will drop rapidly.	Sinking air means there are settled conditions with few clouds and clear skies. Lack of cloud cover allows daily temperatures to be increased but at night the heat will escape back into the atmosphere and temperatures will drop rapidly.
Wind speed and direction	Isobars can be close together and bring strong winds. Winds blow in an anticlockwise direction. A depression usually passes in a NE direction and will take between three to five days to pass over the UK.	Isobars are far apart which indicates light winds and calm conditions. Wind direction is clockwise around the high pressure.	Isobars are far apart which indicates light winds and calm conditions. Wind direction is clockwise around the high pressure.
Precipitation	Precipitation will vary, including snow in winter and a lot of rain over a three to five day period. As the cold front passes, this can bring thunderstorms and lightning (especially in the summer).	There is little or no precipitation during the day but clear skies can bring dew and fog, especially in the mornings. Thunderstorms can be triggered on hot days as convectional rainfall.	There will be very little direct precipitation in a winter anticyclone, however, the rapid loss of heat means that nights can be very cold and temperatures will dip below freezing. Condensation caused by temperature inversions can cause fog and frost.

The limitations of forecasting

Range: The UKMET weather model can help to predict the weather for up to six days in advance.

Accuracy: No weather forecast model can be 100% accurate as there are far too many variables. The surfaces that the weather passes over, the temperature, the microclimate and the size of a settlement can all influence the local weather.

Evaluate the effects (positive and negative) of depressions and anticyclones on the economy and people

Our temperate climate in the British Isles is very unlikely to have truly 'extreme' weather, yet the weather can have both a positive and negative effect on us.

The effects that weather systems can have on people and the economy

Weather System	Positive/ Negative	Effects on people	Effects on the economy
Depressions	Positive	• Depressions bring warmer weather in the winter. • They can bring water during the summer months when there might be drought conditions.	• Depressions bring water, needed for crops. • Clouds keep temperatures above freezing, allowing animals to remain outside for longer and increasing the length of the growing season.
	Negative	• Depressions bring long periods of 'bad' weather and rain which can limit outdoor activities. • Often one depression is followed by another, extending bad weather further.	• As depressions pass, the high wind speeds can cause damage to crops which will cost farmers money. • Strong winds can cause the cancellation of flights and ferries, disrupting transport. This can affect supermarkets and other businesses if stock arrival is delayed.
Summer anticyclones	Positive	• Summer anticyclones bring 'good' weather which can have a positive effect on people, such as encouraging outdoor activities and generally improving people's mood.	• Anticyclones bring weather that allows crops to ripen. • Long periods of anticyclonic weather can help the local tourism industry.
	Negative	• Summer anticyclones bring long periods of heat and dry weather which can increase the chance of drought, hosepipe bans and lead to soil erosion.	• If an anticyclone stays for a long period of time, it can bring drought, which can spoil crops, causing farmers to lose money. Food prices will also increase. • Irrigation can be a solution, however, it is expensive and can damage the soil if not managed carefully.
Winter anticyclones	Positive	• Winter anticyclones can bring nice, clear, crisp days in the winter, providing a break from the wind and rain in a depression. • They can bring freezing temperatures, which can help to remove bugs and bacteria in the soil that otherwise may have damaged crops.	• In winter anticyclones generally only hinder the economy (see negative).

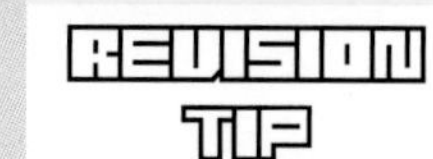

Don't forget, to 'evaluate' you need to make sure that you look at both the positive and negative features before you come to a final decision. In this case you should explain the different ways that each of the weather systems can operate. For example, you might want to consider the impact on different groups of people, such as older people, sports players, healthcare managers and events organisers.

Weather System	Positive/ Negative	Effects on people	Effects on the economy
	Negative	• People with respiratory problems like asthma find it more difficult to breathe in the very cold weather. • Increased amounts of frost and ice can cause a hazard for older people, as they can slip and fall on the ice or suffer when heating fails.	• Temperature inversions can cause heavy fog, which can restrict transport, especially aircraft. • Ice and winter conditions on the roads can cause traffic accidents, which can slow down the movement of goods during the winter. • Older people might find it difficult and expensive to heat their homes in particularly cold spells of weather.

TEST YOUR REVISION

1. State the meaning of the term 'depression'.
2. Describe the formation of a depression.
3. Describe the main features of a depression (pressure, temperature, cloud cover, wind speed and direction, and precipitation).
4. How does an anticyclone form?
5. Describe the main features of an anticyclone (pressure, temperature, cloud cover, wind speed and direction, and precipitation).
6. What are the main differences between a summer and a winter anticyclone?
7. Evaluate the impact of a winter anticyclone on people.

PART 3

THE CAUSES AND CONSEQUENCES OF CLIMATE CHANGE

The difference between the greenhouse effect and global warming

The greenhouse effect

This is when thermal radiation from the surface of the earth is 'bounced' back again due to the 'greenhouse gases' (water vapour, carbon dioxide, methane, nitrous oxide, CFCs and ozone). As a result, the temperature that surrounds the atmosphere will increase.

How greenhouse gases help keep the earth a little warmer than normal:

4. The greenhouse gases that are in the atmosphere trap this infra-red (IR) radiation and the heat is reflected back towards the earth.

1. The sun gives off energy in the form of visible light and ultra-violet (UV) radiation, which travels towards the earth.

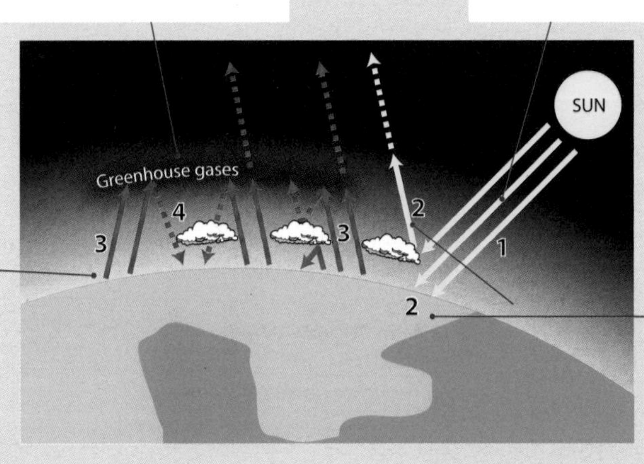

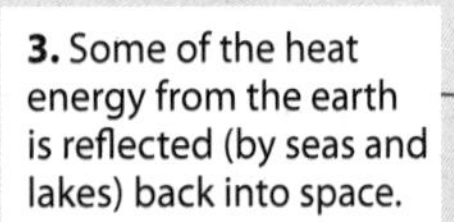

2. Some of the energy is absorbed by the atmosphere, some is absorbed by the earth and some is reflected by clouds back into space. The rest of the energy helps to heat the surface of the earth.

Global warming

This is the name given to the process where the average temperature around the earth is rising. The greenhouse effect is one reason for the rise in global temperature but there are also other causes. The IPCC (the Intergovernmental Panel on Climate Change) indicated in 2007 that during the twenty-first century the global surface temperature is likely to rise between 1.1°C to a possible 6.4°C.

What are the causes of climate change?

NATURAL CAUSES

1. Natural climatic cycles

- Slow changes to the earth's orbit can cause changes to the seasons over a long period of time. The earth's orbit varies and becomes more elongated every 100,000 years and this is linked to the earth's glacial cycles.
- The sun can affect temperature changes, as it is not always constant. Some scientists link the warming of the first half of the twentieth century to an increase in the output of solar energy.

2. Volcanic activity (sulphates and sulphur dioxide)

When volcanoes erupt they send large amounts of sulphate gas, ash and dust (called aerosols) high into the atmosphere. When the tiny particles of sulphur mix with water vapour in the atmosphere this can produce sulphuric acid, which can reflect sunlight back into space. It also creates more sulphur dioxide.

HUMAN CAUSES

1. Burning fossil fuels (carbon dioxide)

Carbon is the main fuel in 'fossil fuels' (coal, oil and natural gas), which are the main sources of energy over the world. When carbon is burned in the air, carbon dioxide is created as a by-product. Many scientists agree that carbon dioxide makes a big contribution to the increase in greenhouse gases and the greenhouse effect.

2. Motor vehicle pollutants (nitrous oxide and hydrocarbons)

Most cars burn oil which helps to make up to about 20% of all carbon emissions within the EU. However, cars and other forms of transport are also responsible for the production of hydrocarbons, nitrogen oxide and nitrogen dioxide.

Evaluate the effects (actual and potential) of climate change on the environment, society and the economy

Effect of climate change	Actual effects	Potential effects
On the environment	• *Increasing temperatures:* The global temperature has risen by 0.75 °C in the last century. • *Increasing rainfall:* Rainfall patterns are changing. Wet places are getting wetter and dry areas are getting drier. • *Glacier and icecap melt:* Polar icecaps and glaciers are melting at a faster rate. Some evidence shows that sea-ice in the Arctic has retreated by 20%. • *Sea level changes:* Since 1900, sea levels around the UK have risen by 10 cm. As water is released from storage in ice, the amount of water in the world's oceans will continue to rise.	• *Plants and animals:* As changes occur to the climate, some species will be unable to adapt. Large areas of rainforest (like the Amazon) will be lost to drought or uncontrolled fire. Polar bears in the Arctic are at risk as they have to swim further between flows of ice, using up more energy, losing weight and bodyfat, resulting in fewer surviving. • *Sea level rise:* The release of water from ice and snow could raise sea levels around the world by up to 5 m. Even a rise of 1 m could flood 25% of Bangladesh.

Effect of climate change	Actual effects	Potential effects
On society	• *Food supply:* The impact on crops and food supply will vary across the world but as climate changes, farmers will need to change crops and farming practices. • *Healthcare:* There will be serious consequences for millions who do not have the ability to adapt to climate change. Malnutrition will increase and more people will die due to extreme weather events such as drought, floods, storms, heatwaves and fires.	• *Availability of water:* It is likely that there will be less water available for drinking or irrigation as rain becomes more valuable with a higher chance of drought conditions. • *Mortality rates in LEDCs:* It is thought that death rates will increase in the future, seriously affecting 660 million people. The total cost to the global economy caused by these deaths could be nearly £220 billion per year.
On the economy	• *Farming:* Traditional farming patterns are being disrupted. It is more difficult for farmers to work in marginal areas (across Africa and South America) and soil erosion is on the rise. • *Flooding:* Damage caused by the flooding of rivers and coasts is increasing. The more water flowing across the surface, the higher the risk of flooding to industrial and economic areas. • *Travel:* Airlines have introduced levies on travellers to help reduce their 'carbon footprint'. They will need to pay more for any pollution caused by their travel.	• *GDP:* The cost of climate change could be huge. Some reports suggest that between 5–20% of global GDP will be used on taking action. • *Flooding:* The impact of flooding on cities and on farmers will continue to worsen in both MEDCs and LEDCs. • *Tourism:* Travel is becoming more expensive which means that less people will travel overseas on holiday.

The UK (a case study from a MEDC to illustrate the effects of climate change)

CASE STUDY

Location: UK

Some of the actual effects of climate change in the UK.

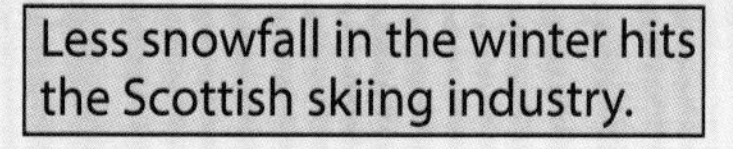

More intense rainfall will further increase the number of houses at risk of flooding.

UK riverside communities will become more used to regular flooding events.

Warmer, wetter winters are disrupting ecosystems in cold, upland areas.

Higher farming yields.

Rising sea levels will flood low lying coastal areas.

The 22 million homes across the UK will need to be adapted to help cope with a 4°C rise in average temperature.

Increase in numbers of insects and pests.

Supplying water to cities will get more expensive as rainfall decreases.

Hotter summers will bring health risks and make travel and city life slower and harder.

In southern England warmer summers bring opportunities for new crops for farmers.

Hosepipe bans and water shortages become a more common feature of British life.

Effects on: Environment Society Economy

Evaluate the potential effects of climate change in the UK

	Environment	Society	Economy
Sea level rises	Coastal areas will be flooded. Their ecosystems will not have enough time to adapt to climate changes and some species will become extinct (eg in the salt marshes of Norfolk).	Homes in low lying areas will be flooded if new coastal defences are not built (eg Belfast and areas around Strangford Lough).	Flood defences can be extremely expensive to build and maintain (over £20 million of government spending per year).
Warmer temperatures	As temperatures rise, both winters and summers will be warmer. Rare arctic plants and alpines will find it more difficult to survive (eg in upland areas of Scotland).	There could be an increase in the influx of insects. Cold winters kill off insect larvae and keep insect numbers manageable.	The warmer, drier conditions will suit some crops (eg wheat, maize and fruit).
Extreme weather (reduced rainfall)	New species of plants will be able to establish themselves (eg grapes could be grown in the south of England).	Droughts will lead to water shortages. People will have to monitor and pay more for the water that they use and hose pipe bans will become more common.	Arable crop farmers will have to invest a lot more money into expensive irrigation systems. Water will be an increasingly valuable resource.

TEST YOUR REVISION

1. What is the difference between the greenhouse effect and global warming?
2. Describe two natural causes of climate change in the atmosphere.
3. Evaluate the effect of climate change on the environment.
4. Evaluate the effect of climate change on one country.

Evaluate the sustainability of strategies to deal with climate change

In recent years there have been a number of strategies used to try and encourage people to take action and start dealing with climate change.

Renewable energy: This is energy that can be used more than once and can be generated without causing pollution or damage to the environment.

Strategy 1: International Agreements (such as the Kyoto Protocol)

International strategy meetings have existed since 1979. The most famous (COP3) took place in Kyoto, Japan, in December 1997. This set out the greenhouse gas emissions reduction obligation for many MEDCs worldwide, where they agreed to reduce greenhouse gases by 6–8% by 2012.

Strategy 2: The use of alternative energy sources (wind power, solar power and biofuels)

Many governments around the world are starting to turn to alternative energy sources to cope with climate change and the dwindling supplies of fossil fuels.

Alternative energy source	Advantages	Disadvantages
Wind power: is a renewable energy which uses the force of the wind to turn the sails on a turbine to generate power.	• It uses a naturally occurring, free source of energy. • It produces no greenhouse gases. • It is sustainable and turbines can last for a very long time – producing cheap, clean energy.	• Wind can be unpredictable – some days will be calm and others can be too windy for the turbines to turn. • Turbines can be costly to build (over £600,000) and it can take some time to reclaim the cost outlay.
Solar power: is a renewable energy which converts the sun's heat and light into electricity.	• It uses a naturally occurring, free source of energy. • It produces no pollution.	• Solar energy cannot work at night and it can be difficult to store. • Solar power stations are expensive to build and solar panels can be expensive to install.
Biofuel: is a renewable energy that can be created using fermented animal or plant waste. It is also known as biogas and biomass.	• It uses a naturally occurring, free source of energy. • It helps dispose of waste products on farms, rubbish dumps, etc. • People can produce and use their own biofuel on a very small scale.	• It can be expensive to set up. • Biogas contains greenhouse gases that can cause climate change. • Production of biofuel oil can involve a huge amount of land, which means less land in agriculture being cultivated for food.

Strategy 3: Cutting down the use of private cars (investing in public transport and congestion charging)

1. **Investing in public transport:** Public transport is seen as a cheap, fast, reliable and environmentally friendly mode of transport. Ballymena firm Wrightbus have introduced a new range of 'Routemaster' buses that operate as both diesel and hybrid electric engines in London to reduce greenhouse gas emissions further.
2. **Congestion charging:** Most congestion charging schemes were not originally intended to deal with climate change but to manage the amount of traffic in the city. In London, drivers pay £10 each time they enter the congestion charging zone in central London. Traffic levels are now 15% lower and there has been a 6% increase in bus passengers.

Strategy 4: Slowing the rate of deforestation in tropical rainforests (and encouraging sustainable practices)

Deforestation: is the cutting down of trees on a large scale and has long been linked with climate change.

- The main method of removal in tropical rainforest is to burn the trees. This releases carbon into the atmosphere and causes an increase in carbon dioxide levels (a greenhouse gas).
- Trees take in carbon dioxide and give back oxygen. Fewer trees means that less carbon dioxide will be recycled.

The Malaysian government tries to use some of the following sustainable methods of logging, as opposed to clearfelling (where everything is removed from the area):

- **Selective cutting:** when single or grouped trees are selected for cutting allowing a natural regeneration of the forest to take place.
- **Integrated cutting:** when several different types of tree are removed at the same time.
- **Strip cutting:** trees are cut down along the path of contours in the land. This can help to stop soil erosion but still clearfells vast strips of land.

Identify the issues and analyse the challenges associated with securing international co-operation to deal with climate change

- Some governments and scientists believe that climate change is simply a natural process.
- Many countries find it difficult to set aside their own national interest, as reducing greenhouse gases may cost a country a lot of money and damage their economy.
- Some governments do not see climate change as a priority. They feel it is more important to improve standards of living and spend money on schools or hospitals.

TEST YOUR REVISION

1. How have international agreements helped to deal with climate change?
2. Evaluate the positives and negatives of using one type of alternative energy to deal with climate change.
3. Describe and explain how cutting down the use of private cars can make climate change more sustainable.
4. Describe how slowing deforestation can make a difference to climate change.
5. Why has it been so difficult to get international agreement in order to deal with the issues of climate change?

1C THE RESTLESS EARTH

1. Basic Rock Types
2. Plate Tectonics Theory
3. Tectonic Activity in the British Isles
4. Earthquakes: Can they be Managed?

PART 1

BASIC ROCK TYPES

Rock is a solid, natural mass of mineral matter which makes up the crust of our earth and is divided into three types:

Igneous rocks (basalt and granite): are formed due to the cooling and solidification of molten rock (magma) from underneath the earth's crust.

Sedimentary rocks (limestone and sandstone): are formed by the sediments that have built up over a long period of time, usually under water.

Metamorphic rocks (slate and marble): are rocks that have been changed from an earlier state through the addition of pressure or heat.

REVISION TIP

Make sure that you know the key facts in relation to the three different types of rock and can identify examples.

PART

PLATE TECTONICS THEORY

The structure of the earth

The theory of plate tectonics helps us to understand what is happening beneath our feet. The distance from the edge of the crust to the centre of earth is 6,370 km.

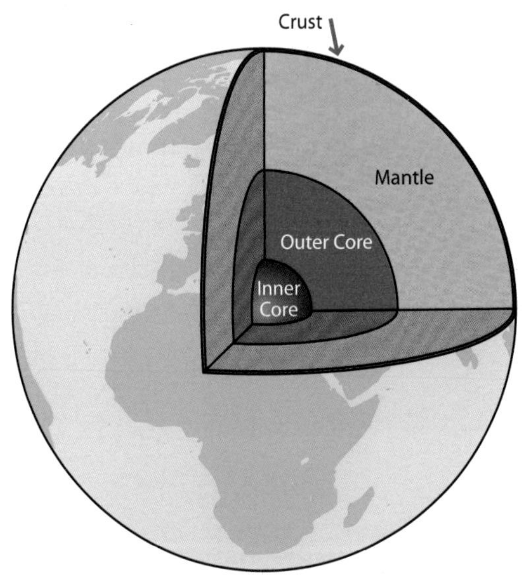

The structure of the earth

The crust: is the thin layer in the outermost section of the earth. It varies between 5–70 km in depth and is broken up into several large pieces of rock which are known as plates.

The core: is at the centre of the earth, with temperatures of over 6,000 °C. The material here is much more dense than at the crust. The outer core is 1,200 km deep and the inner core is 2,200 km deep.

The mantle: is the thickest layer of the earth (at 2,900 km). It is made up of silicate rocks that remain molten and can move about.

The earth's crust, plates and movement

Hard crustal rock seems to sit on a layer of liquid, molten mantle rock. Scientists have noted that increased tectonic activity (earthquakes or volcanoes) takes place in zones of activity, which are located at the boundaries or margins of plates.

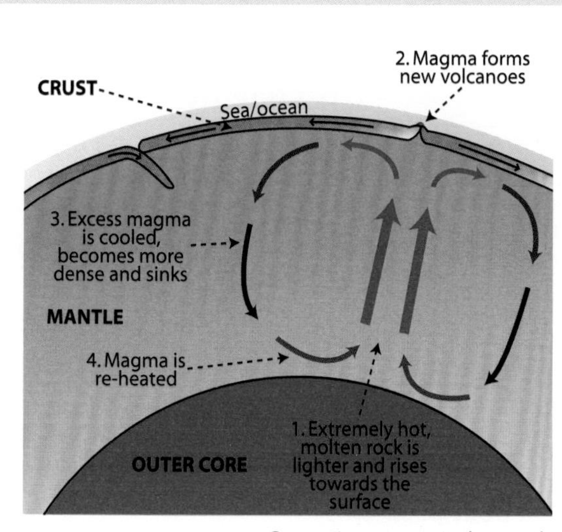

Convection currents in the mantle

How convection currents cause plate movement

1. Inside the thick layer of mantle, the rock melts. As the rock becomes liquid, it becomes less dense than the material above it and it starts to rise towards the surface.
2. The molten rock (magma) rises and attempts to break through cracks in the crust.
3. Any excess magma starts to cool and solidify.
4. As the rock becomes denser, it sinks back deeper into the mantle, where it becomes heated again.

Plate types

Plates are the large sections of rock which make up the crust of the earth. There are two different types of plate:

Continental Plates	Oceanic Plates
• 35–100 km (thick) • Form at land masses/continental areas • Rocks can be very old • Generally contains 'light' rocks that are less dense • *Example:* Granite	• 6–10 km (thin) • Form at the bottom of ocean floors • Rocks can be very young • Generally contains 'heavy' rocks that are more dense • *Example:* Basalt

There are seven major plates (North American, Pacific, South American, Antarctic, African, Eurasian and the Indo-Australia plates) and other minor plates (which include the Nazca, Cocos, Caribbean, Arabian and Philippine).

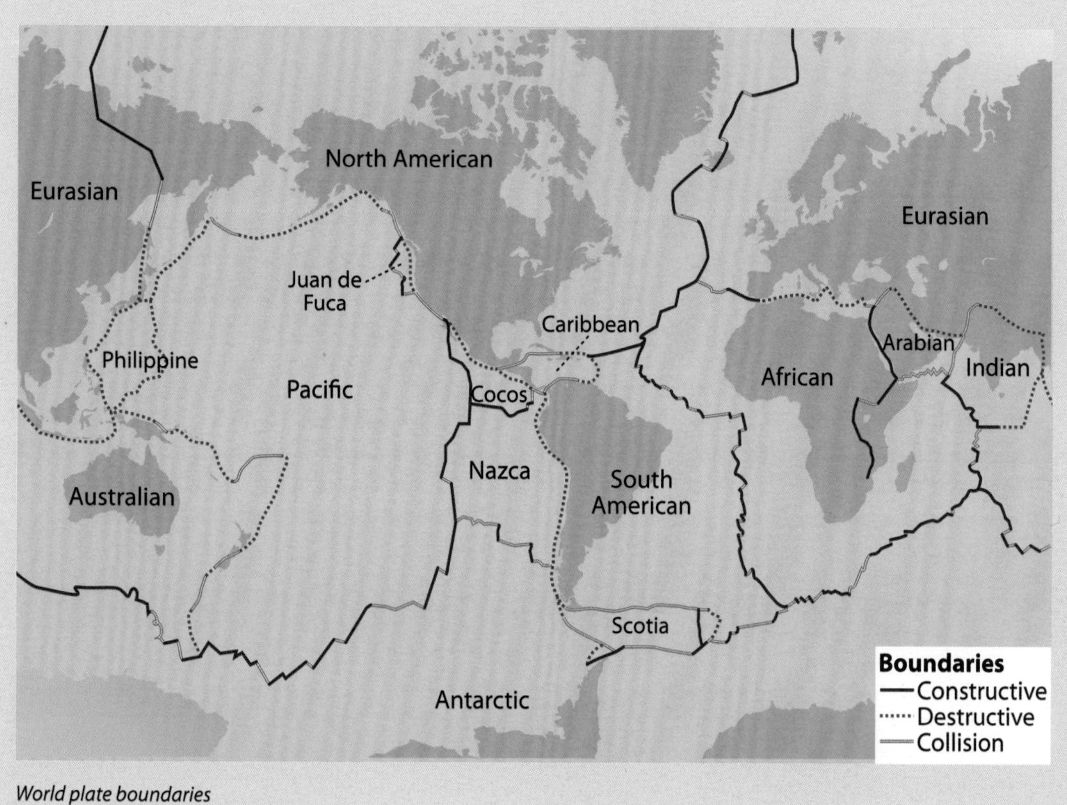

World plate boundaries

Plate margin/ boundary: This is the place where two plates meet. Plates rarely move at consistent speeds. Some plates move regularly whilst others have not moved in centuries.

The processes and landforms associated with plate margins

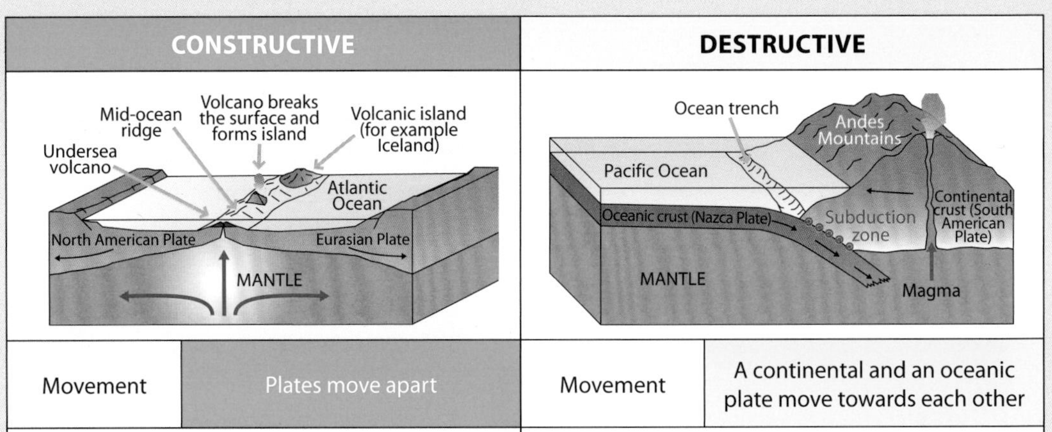

CONSTRUCTIVE

Movement	Plates move apart

Description

As the two pates move away from each other, they create a gap in the seabed (mid-ocean ridge) which is filled with fresh material from deep inside the earth.

Undersea volcanoes are formed, some of which continue to grow with every eruption until they form small islands.

When plates move, this can sometimes trigger earthquakes.

Landform	Mid-ocean ridge
Example	Iceland

DESTRUCTIVE

Movement	A continental and an oceanic plate move towards each other

Description

Plates move because of convection currents in the mantle.

Denser, heavier oceanic crust plate moves towards the lighter but thicker continental crust plate and the oceanic plate is forced underneath.

This creates a deep ocean trench with the movement creating a subduction zone, where earthquakes can be felt.

As the oceanic plate sinks, the plate is heated by the mantle and begins to melt, putting pressure on the magma chamber and causing violent volcanic eruptions and composite cone volcanoes.

Landform	Subduction zone and ocean trench
Example	Nevado del Ruiz and the Andes

COLLISION

Movement	Two continental plates move towards each other

Description

Two plates are forced by convection currents in the mantle to move towards each other. The plates push each other upwards.

Sometimes violent earthquakes can signal plate movement.

Fold mountains can be made from sedimentary rock. The plates then move towards each other and the rock is crumpled upwards to form the folded mountains. When the rock is folded upwards it is called an anticline and when it is folded downwards it is a syncline.

Landform	Fold mountains
Example	Himalayas

CONSERVATIVE

Movement	Two plates are slipping past each other

Description

The plates do not pass each other smoothly. There is a lot of friction between the two plates, which can build up over time.

When the pressure of the friction is released to allow the plate to move, the plate will be 'jerked' forward and the momentum can cause an earthquake.

Landform	Fault lines
Example	San Andreas Fault, California

REVISION TIP

Exam questions will require that you clearly show detailed knowledge of the four different types of plate margin/boundary. You should learn the reasons for the plate movement and how this causes particular tectonic movements.

TEST YOUR REVISION

1. What are the three main rock types?
2. Explain how metamorphic rocks are formed.
3. What are some of the main features of the core and crust?
4. How can convection currents cause plates to move?
5. What is the difference between continental and oceanic plates?
6. Explain the tectonic activity at a constructive plate margin.

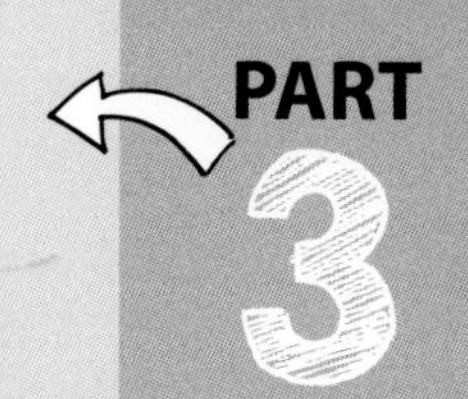

TECTONIC ACTIVITY IN THE BRITISH ISLES

Identify landscape features created by tectonic activity and explain their formation

Previously Northern Ireland was located on the edge of the Eurasian Plate but continued activity at this constructive plate boundary has gradually pushed Ireland further away from the North American Plate. This means that today there is very little tectonic activity taking place in Northern Ireland, and the volcanic features are extinct.

Lava plateau (for example, Antrim Plateau)

Lava plateaus are extrusive features which are formed when a series of basalt lava flows build up on top of each other. Three major flows of volcanic activity formed the Antrim Plateau and allowed it to spread as far north as the North Coast and as far south as the edge of Belfast (to Cave Hill and Carnmoney Hill).

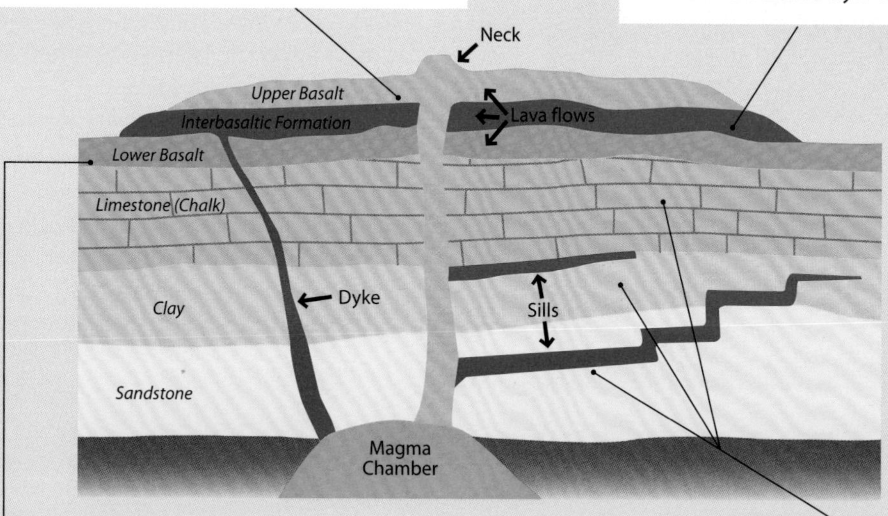

4. The final period of tectonic activity brought further lava flows to the surface through fissures and formed the cap of the Antrim Plateau.

3. As lava flows continued due to increased volcanic activity, the interbasaltic layer was left.

2. Volcanic activity brought dust and fragmented rock which became the lower basalt. Further volcanic activity brought lava flows, which came through cracks and fissures in the ground.

1. Originally the area was covered in old layers of sandstone, clay and limestone.

Volcano: A volcano is a vent in the ground which is caused by the upward movement of magma through cracks in the rock.

Extrusive: This feature is formed above the earth's surface when magma flows out onto the surface as lava and igneous rock remains.

Intrusive: This feature occurs below the earth's surface, when the magma does not reach the surface.

Basalt columns (for example, Giant's Causeway)

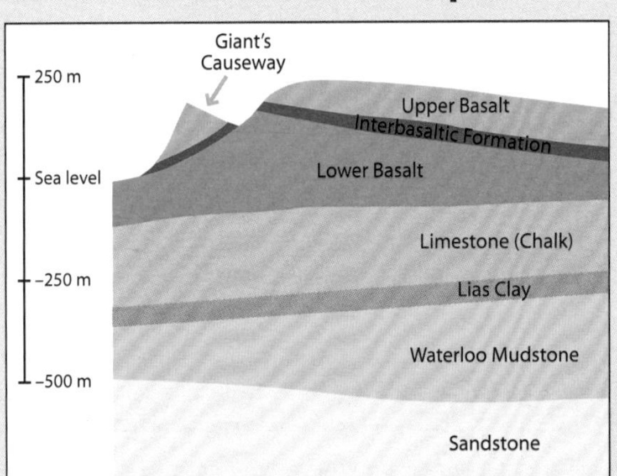

The Giant's Causeway is an extrusive feature caused because the cooling conditions for basalt were perfect. Geologists believe that the columns occurred when lava erupted (from the Carrickarede fissure) into an ancient river valley where the lava became trapped and cooled very slowly.

As the lava started to cool, cracks appeared on the surface and the lava lost heat upwards into the atmosphere. Tension caused by different rates of cooling and shrinking within the columns split the columns into regular tablets of stone. The hexagonal shape was the most efficient way to fill a space.

Volcanic plugs (for example, Slemish Mountain)

Slemish Mountain is one of the largest dolerite plugs in the Antrim Plateau. It rises to 437 m above sea level on the south side of the Braid Valley, about 4 miles from Broughshane.

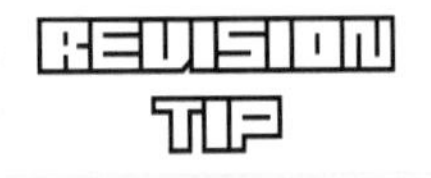

It is common for exam questions to ask candidates to describe the formation of tectonic features. Make sure that you can explain how these are formed.

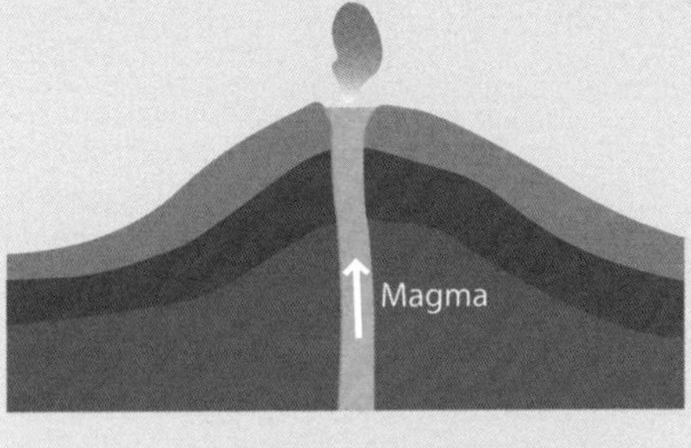

1. Volcanic plugs are intrusive features, formed when magma is forced up from under the crust to move up inside the vent of a volcano.

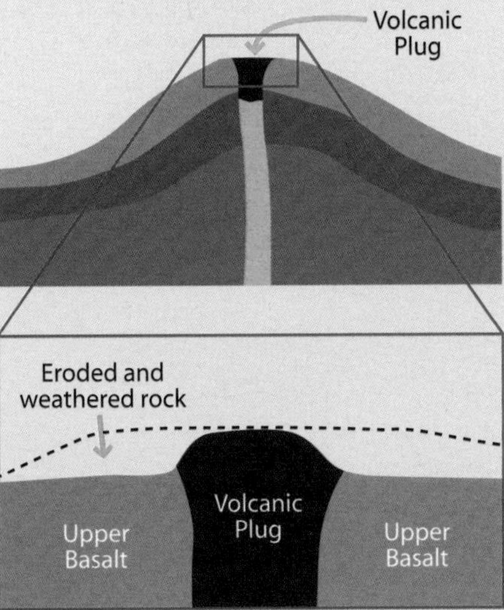

2. As volcanic activity ends the vent is blocked by a lump of hardened magma, which forms rock called dolerite. Dolerite is similar to basalt but it is cooled a little more slowly, and is harder and more resistant to erosion.

3. Over time rain, ice and wind weathers away the softer basalt slopes of the volcano, leaving the harder dolerite exposed above the flat landscapes of the Antrim Plateau.

Describe and explain the cause and impact of an earthquake in the British Isles

The British Isles are no longer positioned on the edge of a plate boundary. Any earthquakes that occur are to do with old, shallow fault lines settling in the rocks, rather than deep tectonic activity.

The intensity of the Market Rasen earthquake felt across the British Isles

Case Study: The Market Rasen earthquake, 27 February 2008

Date:	27 February 2008
Location:	approx 2½ miles north of Market Rasen (Lincolnshire, England)
Magnitude:	5.2 on the Richter scale
Depth:	12 miles
Lasted:	approx 10 seconds

Causes

This earthquake was not caused by plate movement. However, tectonic pressures from the North Atlantic ridge on the African Plate caused stress which led to a sudden rupture along the strike slip fault line in the local area.

Impact

The impact of this earthquake was relatively minor:

- Some buildings were reported to shake for 30 seconds.
- There was some structural damage – roofs collapsed and chimney pots fell from a few houses.
- Birds and pets became agitated and 77 hens died in Pete Sargent's shed.
- There were no deaths but David Bates suffered a fractured pelvis when a chimney smashed through the roof and landed on him as he lay in bed.
- The spire at St Mary Magdalene Church at Waltham was also damaged.
- The estimated cost of the damage was around £10 million.

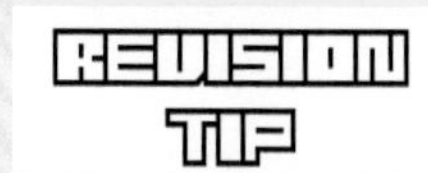

It can be tricky to write long answers about the causes of earthquakes in the British Isles. Make sure that you fully understand the main impacts of this earthquake.

EARTHQUAKES: CAN THEY BE MANAGED?

The global distribution and causes of earthquakes in relation to plate boundaries

An **earthquake** is described as a "fault rupture that generates seismic waves". This occurs when rocks on either side of a weakness in the earth's crust (a fault) cause the ground to vibrate and shake.

The **epicentre** is the place on the earth's surface which is the shortest distance from the focus. It is where the intensity or the magnitude of the energy released is felt the most.

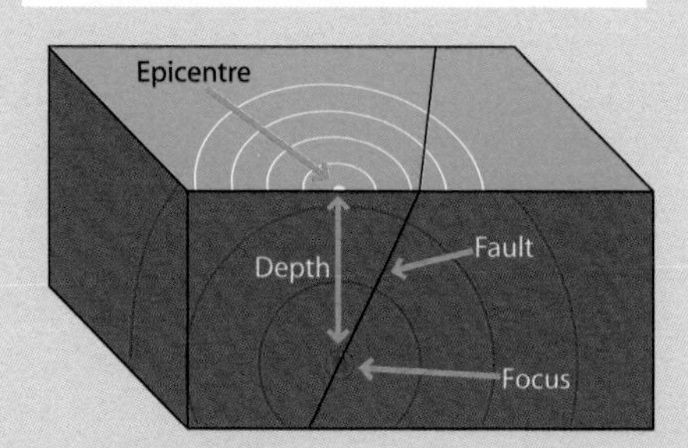

The strength of an earthquake (its magnitude) is measured on the Richter Scale. This is a logarithmic scale, which means that a magnitude 6.0 earthquake is 10 times greater than a magnitude 5.0 earthquake.

The seismic waves (vibrations) travel from the **focus** (the place where the earthquake originally occurs) to the surface.

Seismic waves can be recorded using a **seismograph** (a weight with a pen attached, which is suspended from a spring).

There is a clear global pattern for earthquakes around the world. Major earthquakes occur in zones of activity which coincide with the different plate boundaries that are spread across the surface of the earth. Generally:

- earthquakes occur in narrow belts on plate margins.
- they occur on all four types of plate margins.
- the most powerful earthquakes are associated with destructive, collision and conservative plate margins.
- earthquakes at constructive plate boundaries tend to be weaker.

The physical consequences of earthquakes

Liquefaction

Liquefaction occurs when an earthquake hits an area and shakes the wet soil. The shaking causes the water within the soil to start to rise to the surface, and this process turns solid soil and rock into a liquid mud. Buildings will start to sink and tip over as the support for the foundations is waterlogged and cannot maintain the weight of the buildings.

Tsunami

A tsunami is a large wave which is created when an underwater earthquake sends shockwaves through the water, causing a surge of water to move towards the coastline. Often the energy transferred due to a tsunami can travel for thousands of miles across the oceans.

How a tsunami happens

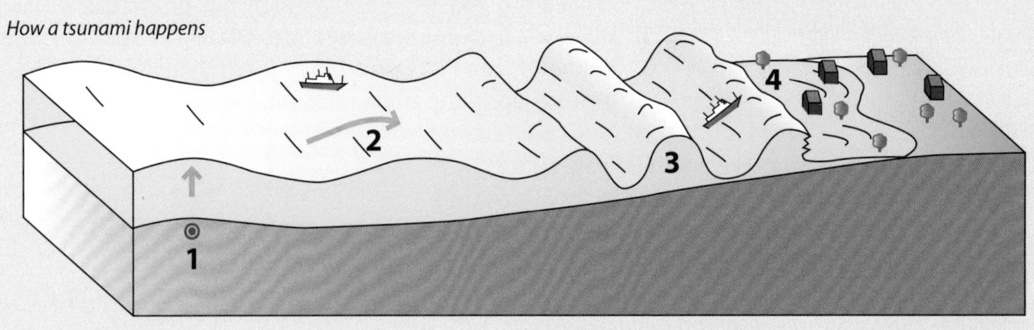

1. A rupture in the sea floor pushes water upwards and starts the waves moving.
2. The waves move rapidly across the deep ocean, reaching speeds of up to 500 km/h.
3. As the waves near land, they slow to 45 km/h but get squeezed upwards by the sloping beach and the waves start to increase in height.
4. The waves climb to 10–40 metres in height and move inland, destroying everything in their way.

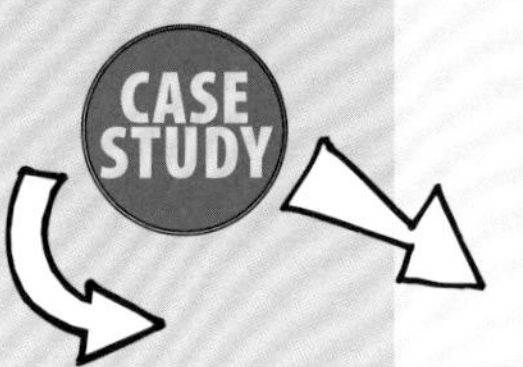

MEDC Case Study: The Great Tohoku earthquake (Japan, 11 March 2011)

Date:	11 March 2011
Time:	14.46
Location:	Off the coast of Japan
Epicentre:	43 miles east of Tohoku
Magnitude:	9.0 undersea earthquake
Depth:	20 miles
Lasted:	6 minutes
Tsunami:	Wave height 40.5 m, travelled 6 miles inland

Causes

- Japan lies on a destructive plate boundary, where both the Philippine and the Pacific Plate (oceanic) are moving towards the Eurasian/North American Plate (continental) at a fairly fast rate.
- A large amount of friction was built up over time, causing the Pacific Plate to be subducted beneath the Eurasion Plate, leading to a megathrust earthquake.

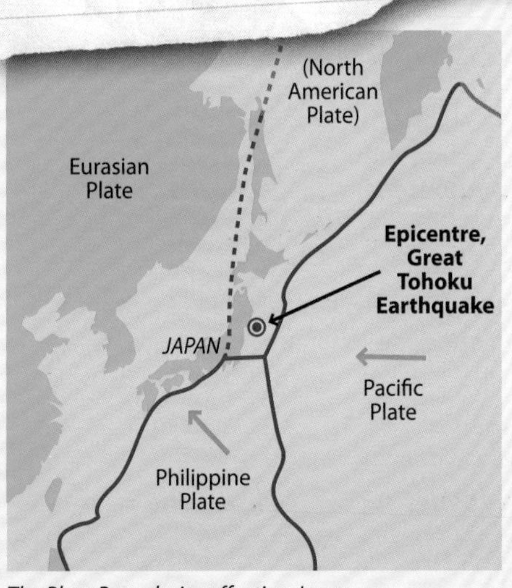

The Plate Boundaries affecting Japan

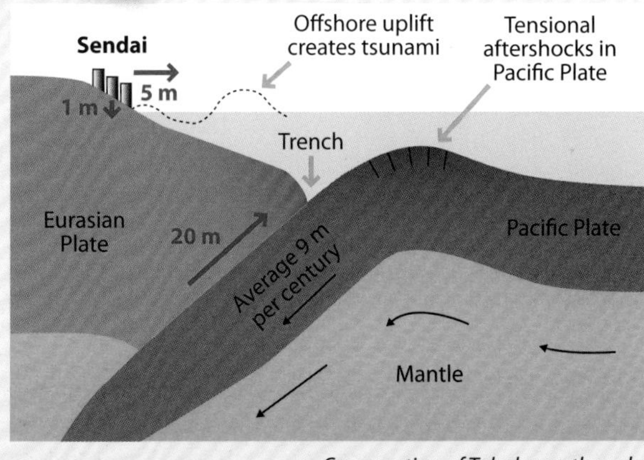

Cross section of Tohoku earthquake

Impacts on people and the environment

Short term impacts (on people and the environment)

ON PEOPLE

1. Death and Injury: 20,352 people died, 5,314 people were injured and 130,927 were displaced.

2. Nuclear crisis: The Fukushima nuclear plant was protected by a 5 m high tsunami barrier, yet a 9 m wave came ashore and flooded the plant's generators.

3. Defences ineffective: Japan had spent billions of dollars on tsunami defences, yet the tsunami washed over them, with water moving up to 6 miles inland, destroying houses, factories and roads.

4. Damage: 332,395 buildings, 2,126 roads, 56 bridges and 26 railways were destroyed or damaged. 300 hospitals were damaged and 11 were destroyed. 23,000 cars and trucks were damaged. Ports were closed for 3 weeks. One dam ruptured and another 6 were found to have cracks.

5. Power supplies: 4.4 million households in NE Japan lost electricity and power blackouts were felt in some areas for up to 3 months.

ON THE ENVIRONMENT

1. Fore and aftershocks: A number of foreshocks were measured (some up to 7.2 on the Richter scale) plus hundreds of aftershocks – three measured more than magnitude 6 and another three at magnitude 7. An estimated 800 earthquakes rocked this area, which created fissures in the ground and caused damage.

2. Tsunami: A 40 m high tsunami was generated which devastated entire towns and resulted in the loss of thousands of lives. The wave also travelled east towards Alaska and Chile. The flooding caused by the waves damaged buildings, caused pollution and affected drinking water.

3. Land subsidence: Some coastal areas experienced subsidence and the beachfront dropped by 50 cm and made the area even more liable to flooding.

Long term impacts (on people and the environment)

ON PEOPLE

1. Economy: The World Bank estimated a cost of US$235 billion for the damage and thought this would take 5 years to rebuild.

2. Tsunami: Only 58% of people living in coastal areas heeded Tsunami warnings to head for higher ground. The water hit almost half of those people who did not heed this warning.

3. Nuclear Energy: Earthquake damage caused the meltdown of 7 reactors, leading to evacuation of areas affecting over 200,000 people. Radiation at one time was 8 times the normal levels. Radioactive water and leaks caused problems in soil and food over a wide area. All the Japanese nuclear reactors were taken offline until June 2012.

4. Transport: Japan's transport network suffered huge disruptions. Sections of the Tohoku expressway were damaged and Sendai airport was hit by the Tsunami wave. Four trains were derailed and 1,100 sections of rail line needed repaired.

ON THE ENVIRONMENT

1. Landmass movement: The quake moved NE Japan 2.4 m closer to N America, making parts of the Japanese island landmass wider than before.

2. Coastline movement: a 250 mile stretch of coastline dropped by 0.6 m, allowing the tsunami wave to travel further inland.

3. Liquefaction: This occurred in many areas. 30 homes were destroyed and 1,046 buildings were damaged in this way.

4. Aftershocks: Japan measured over 900 aftershocks following the earthquake, some of which were over magnitude 7 and caused further death and destruction.

5. Antarctica: Some seismic waves were reported to have caused massive slabs of ice to fall from the Sulzberger Ice shelf.

Evaluation of the management response

Prediction and precautions	
BEFORE the earthquake	**AFTER the earthquake**
Earthquake prediction: Japan has spent over £70 million trying to predict earthquakes before they happen. They use lasers to measure possible earth movements.	**Refugees:** The earthquake created over 300,000 refugees and resulted in shortages of food, water, shelter, medicine and fuel for survivors.
National Disaster Prevention Day: Every year, on 1 September, the Japanese government holds earthquake and tsunami drills.	**Aid:** Aid organisations in Japan and worldwide responded to the disaster. The Japanese Red Cross reported over $1 billion in donations (many from overseas).
Earthquake-proof buildings: Japan spends billions of pounds on buildings that are designed to be resistant to the effects of earthquakes.	**Rebuilding:** The Japanese Government announced that more than 23 trillion Yen over the next 10 years would be made available to aid rebuilding programmes.
Early warning systems: The tsunami warning system in Japan was set up in 1952 with 300 sensors. Tsunami safety has been a focus for coastal city planning throughout the nation. Hundreds of earthquake and tsunami-proof shelters have been built and some cities have built tsunami walls and floodgates to stop waves from travelling inland through river systems.	**Tsunami barriers:** New 18 m high barriers are being built around some of the remaining nuclear power stations.
	Economic factors: Even when some industrialists (such as carmakers Toyota and Honda) wanted to restart production in their factories, they found this difficult to achieve.

REVISION TIP

It is really important that you know the details behind **BOTH** of the earthquake case studies. Make sure that you carefully learn the causes of each of the earthquake events and are able to write in depth about the short and long term impacts on people and the environment.

CASE STUDY

LEDC Case Study: The Haiti earthquake (Haiti, 12 January 2010)

Date:	12 January 2010
Time:	16:53
Location:	16 miles west of Port-au-Prince, Haiti
Epicentre:	Inland
Magnitude:	7.0
Depth:	8 miles

Plate map of the Central America area

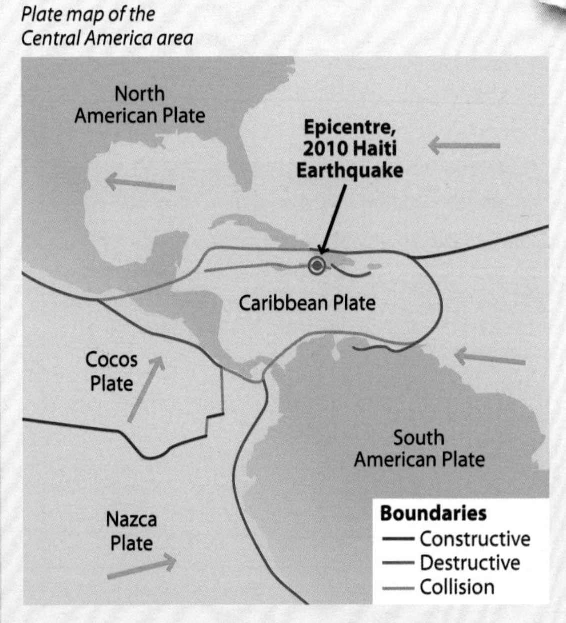

Main Faults involved

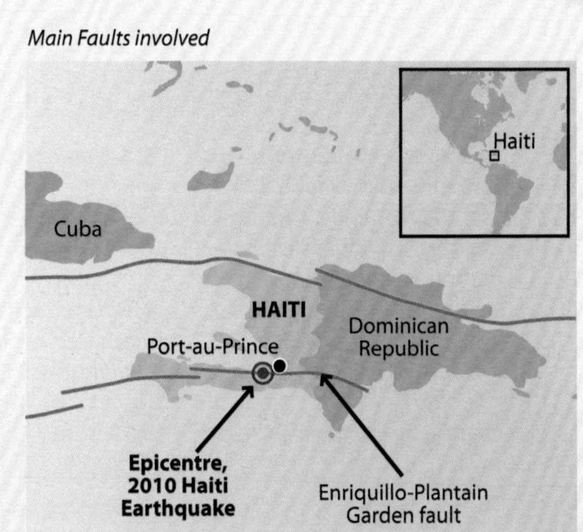

Causes

- Haiti lies at the boundary of the Caribbean and North American Plates, where the Caribbean Plate is moving eastward in a strike-slip (conservative) motion.
- This movement is not smooth and can produce earthquakes.
- The Haiti earthquake is believed to have caused a slip of about 1.8 m but before this there had been little activity in the area for 250 years.

Impacts on people and the environment

Short term impacts (on people and the environment)

ON PEOPLE

1. Location: The earthquake took place very close to the capital city of Haiti (Port-au-Prince) in what is a very densely populated part of the country.

2. Death and injury: An estimated 222,570 died, 300,000 were injured and 1.3 million were displaced.

3. Damage: 97,294 houses were destroyed and 188,383 were damaged in the south of the country. Around 3.5 million people were affected by the quake. More than 1,300 schools were destroyed.

4. Poverty: Haiti was already an exceptionally poor LEDC before this earthquake hit. It was listed as 145th out of 169 countries in the UN Human Development Index.

ON THE ENVIRONMENT

1. Aftershocks: Over the next month, 52 aftershocks measuring magnitude 4.5 or more were recorded in the area, with three reaching magnitude 5.9.

2. Mini-tsunami: A 'mini-tsunami' was reported in the small fishing town of Petit Paradis. Three people were swept out to sea and died, as boats and debris were swept out into the ocean.

3. Location: Much of Port-au-Prince's residential areas were built on hillsides, which collapsed and caused landlsides. Soil and rock were moved by the earthquake due to the deforestation in the area.

Long term impacts (on people and the environment)

ON PEOPLE

1. Industry and employment: The clothing industry accounts for more than two-thirds of Haiti's exports and it was hit severely by the earthquake. An estimated one in every five jobs in Haiti was lost.

2. Homelessness: Many people continued to sleep in the streets, on pavements or in cars after the earthquake, as they were worried that structures would not be able to withstand aftershocks.

3. Aid: The impact of the earthquake meant that it took nearly a week for relief efforts to be organised properly and the government handed over control of the airport and ports to the US to hasten and ease flight operations. Very quickly, even the most basic of medical supplies began to run out (such as antibiotics).

4. Health risks: Many bodies remained unburied for long periods of time and in the heat and humidity, the corpses started to smell and decompose, causing serious health risks to survivors.

ON THE ENVIRONMENT

1. Physical: There were very few impacts on the physical environment caused by this earthquake. Most of the impacts were due to the proximity of this earthquake to a major urban area.

2. Relocation: In April, due to the potential threat of mudslides and flooding from the upcoming rainy season, the Haitian government began operations to move thousands of refugees to a more secure location north of the capital.

3. Out migration: In the months which followed, many people started to return to the rural areas where they had lived and farmed prior to migrating into Haiti before the earthquake.

Evaluation of the management response

Prediction and precautions	
BEFORE the earthquake	**AFTER the earthquake**
Earthquake prediction: Haiti did not have an organised system for predicting or warning people about earthquakes or potential natural disasters.	**Refugees:** Over 3 million people were initially left homeless by the impact of this earthquake. Six months later, the number of people in relief camps of tents and tarps was 1.6 million, and almost no transitional housing had been built. Most of the camps had no electricity, running water or sewage disposal, and the tents were beginning to fall apart. Crime was widespread in these camps.
Buildings: Many of the buildings in Haiti were temporary constructions and not built to withstand the most basic of disasters.	**Aid:** Many countries and international aid organisations mobilised quickly to send emergency aid to Haiti. Disaster relief teams, emergency field hospitals, emergency food supplies, water and materials were all supplied quickly in response to urgent requests for assistance by the Haitian authorities.
Emergency services: The emergency services were unprepared and inadequate for any form of rescue following the disaster. Many more people would have died if international aid organisations and governments had not stepped in when they did.	**Rebuilding:** Six months after the disaster as much as 98% of the rubble from the earthquake remained uncleared. Most of the capital city was still impassable and thousands of bodies remained in the rubble.
	Cholera: In late October 2010 an outbreak of cholera was confirmed in Haiti which required further relief efforts, including emergency supplies, blankets, buckets and disinfectant supplies. Cholera treatment facilities were established to support isolation and treatment for cases, and to prepare for the spread of the disease (which eventually had around 6,000 beds for cholera treatment). By the end of 2010, more than 3,300 had died of Cholera.

TEST YOUR REVISION

1. Explain how a lava plateau is formed.
2. What is the difference between volcanic plugs and basalt columns?
3. What caused the Market Rasen earthquake in 2008?
4. Define 'focus' and 'epicentre'.
5. How can liquefaction happen during an earthquake?
6. Describe the causes of the MEDC earthquake that hit Japan in 2011.
7. Explain two impacts of the MEDC earthquake on people.
8. Describe the causes of the LEDC earthquake that hit Haiti in 2010.
9. Explain two impacts of the LEDC earthquake on the environment.
10. Evaluate the management response towards the earthquake in Haiti in 2010 (LEDC).

Unit 2: Living in Our World

2A PEOPLE AND WHERE THEY LIVE

1. **Population Growth, Change and Structure**
2. **Settlement Site, Function and Hierarchy**
3. **Urbanisation in LEDCs and MEDCs**

POPULATION GROWTH, CHANGE AND STRUCTURE

World population growth since 1700

The study of population is all about the balance that can be achieved through births and deaths.

Graph of the Total World Population over the last 2000 years

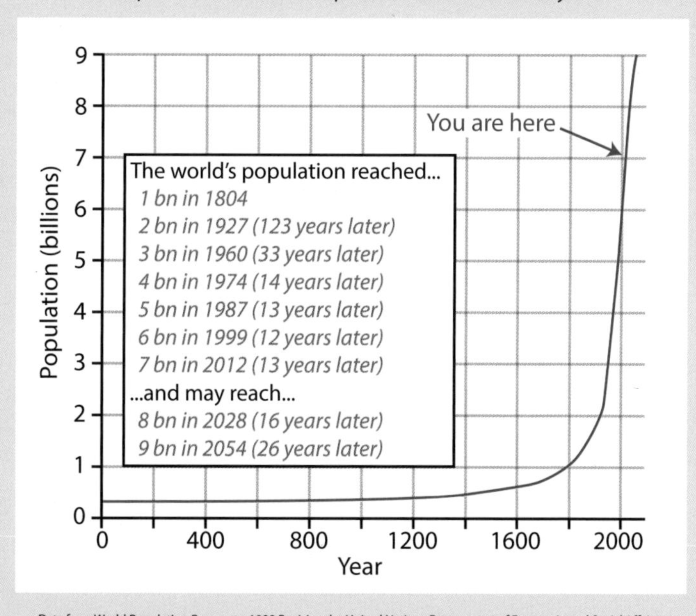

Data from World Population Prospects: 1998 Revision, by United Nations Department of Economic and Social Affairs Population Division, © 2015 United Nations. Reprinted with the permission of the United Nations.

The graph above shows how the world population has changed over time. In many countries the pattern for change began when death rates fell due to improvements in health care. Before this, birth and death rates were both high. Later birth rates also began to fall as society changed. In many MEDCs today, the birth and death rates are both low. In LEDCs the death rates are falling but birth rates remain high.

Birth Rate: (or crude birth rate) is the number of live births each year per thousand of the population in an area.

Death Rate: (or crude death rate) is the number of deaths each year per thousand of the population in an area.

Natural Increase: is when there is a growth in the number of people in an area – the birth rate is higher than the death rate.

Natural Decrease: is when there is a decline in the number of people in an area – the birth rate is lower than the death rate.

The typical changes to birth and death rates in a MEDC are shown in the table below.

Population change over time

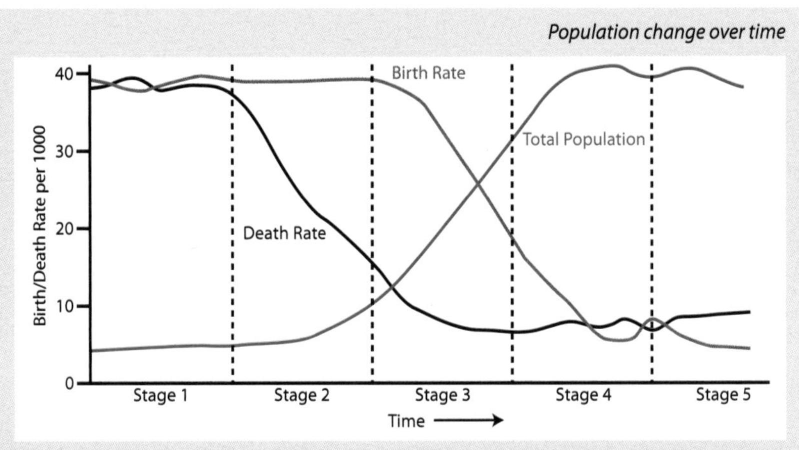

Stage 1 High birth and death rates	Stage 2 Death rates fall	Stage 3 Birth rates fall	Stage 4 Low birth and death rates	Stage 5 Birth rates drop below death rates
Both birth and death rates are high and fluctuate (36/37 per 1,000). Many babies are being born into large families, but they are not surviving and few people are living long lives.	**Birth rates remain high but death rates fall rapidly (to 18/19 per 1,000).** Life expectancy increases and death rates fall. The birth rate remains high and this difference between the two population rates is what begins the population explosion in a country.	**Birth rates fall rapidly (to around 18 per 1,000) to give a slowly increasing population.** The birth rate begins to fall and social and economic pressures produce a reduction in the number of babies born within the country.	**A form of equilibrium occurs within the population.** Both the birth rates (15 per 1,000) and death rates (12 per 1,000) are low and can fluctuate to give a steady population.	Some countries, mostly western European states, can experience a **negative population growth** as the birth rate (7 per 1,000) slips below the death rate (9 per 1,000). This can produce a population which will eventually decline, as the population will not continue to replace itself.
Birth rates are high as: • There is no birth control or family planning. • Many children will die in infancy and parents will have a large number of children to ensure that some reach adulthood. • Many children are needed to work on the land. **Death rates are high due to:** • Disease, famine and poor diet. • Poor hygiene due to a lack of piped water, sewage and basic toilet facilities. • Little medical care, few doctors, hospitals or drugs.	**Death rates fall due to:** • Improved medical care, sanitation and water supplies. • Improvements in food production (both quality and quantity). • A decrease in child mortality.	**Birth rates fall due to:** • An increased use of family planning. • A lower infant mortality rate, which means that children are now surviving through to adulthood and parents do not need to have as many. • Increased industrialisation and mechanisation, which means fewer labourers are needed. • An increased desire for material possessions and a reduced interest in large families.		Population is ageing and is dominated by older people.

Many LEDCs have found that their death rates have fallen rapidly due to the amount of aid they receive from MEDCs. Their healthcare facilities and access to medicine has improved, so life expectancies have increased. Their birth rates remain high but these are also starting to fall as people have wider access to contraception.

TEST YOUR REVISION

1. Describe some of the causes of world population growth.
2. State the meaning of 'birth rate'.
3. Describe what natural increase is.
4. Explain why the death rate might decrease in a developing country.
5. Explain two factors that have led to a falling birth rate.

Skills: Using GIS to investigate in-migration within a MEDC (Northern Ireland)

Geographic Information Systems (GIS) are described by the Ordnance Survey as being "a family of computer software tools that allow information to be linked to a geographical location." GIS stores information in a series of layers. Each layer contains data about a different feature for a location, in the form of maps, graphs and photography. GIS maps allow geographers to interrogate key pieces of information associated with places and compare them to look for patterns and solutions to issues using a map.

Migration is usually planned and often people from the same place will migrate along the same routes and towards the same places as people before them. The place that a migrant leaves is known as the origin and the place where they are intending to move to is called the destination.

Using GIS to investigate migration flows within Northern Ireland

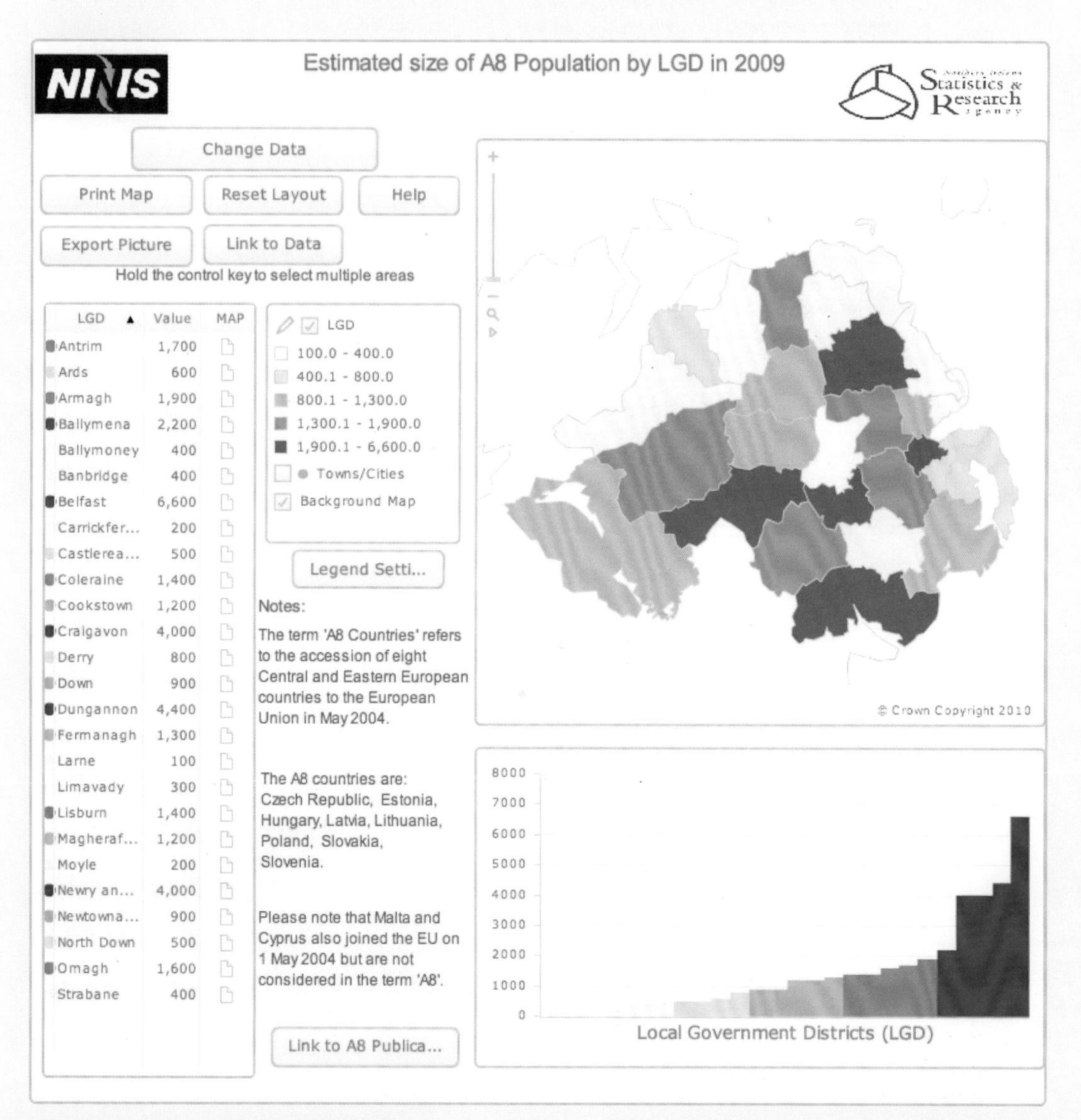

Maps like the one above can be used in an examination so you must be able to read the map and explain where the immigrants are moving to. This map shows the 'Estimated size of A8 population by LGD in 2009'. This is information from the NINIS (Northern Ireland Neighbourhood Information Service), which provides statistical information for Northern Ireland.

Migration: is the movement of people from one place to another. It can take place over short or long distances and can be a permanent one-way movement or it may be temporary.

Immigration: This is when people move into a country.

Emigration: is when people are leaving or exiting a country.

Forced migration: is when a migrant has no personal choice in the decision to move. This is caused by push factors.

Voluntary migration: is when a migrant makes a 'free choice' to move. This is caused by pull factors.

Push factors: These are factors that make people want to leave an area, such as natural disasters, economic problems and war.

Pull factors: These are factors that attract a person to an area, such as looking for a better life, a better standard of living and more personal freedom.

International migration: is when people move from one country to another country internationally.

CASE STUDY

The positive and negative impacts of international migration

Case Study: International migration from Turkey to Germany

Immigration into Germany reached its peak in the 1990s. The 2010 population figures showed that Germany had the highest number of foreign-born citizens in the EU (close to 10 million people and making up 12% of their population).

Many Turkish workers made the decision to travel to Germany and become a guest worker. In 2010 the German embassy estimated that there were about 4 million Turks in Germany. The table below helps to identify some of the main impacts that migration movements can have on the economy and services.

	Positive Impact on Origin (Turkey)	Positive Impact on Destination (Germany)	Negative Impact on Origin (Turkey)	Negative impact on Destination (Germany)
Impact on the economy	• More people leaving Turkey takes the pressure off the unemployment rate. • More money comes back into the economy as remittances. • Most guest workers only spend a few years working in Germany – when they return they bring more money and more skills.	• Turkish immigrants provided a cheap, skilled workforce, which assisted the labour shortage following the Second World War. • The increased cheap labour allowed rapid expansion of German manufacturing.	• The people who migrate are often the more educated and skilled workers, so the country experiences a 'brain drain'. • The people who are left are less skilled and therefore productivity and innovation declines.	• In 1967 and 1990 recession led to unemployment. Many Germans lost their jobs but the Turks remained in their low paid jobs – this fuelled social and ethnic conflict in some cities.
Impact on services	• As people leave Turkey this can reduce the pressure on services, allowing the government to concentrate on essential services.	• The Turkish people usually take on jobs that the Germans do not want to do. Many of these provide low cost personal services (eg hairdressing, cleaning and driving buses) for the German population.	• With many of the economically active people leaving, this might cause a reduction in services.	• More money is spent on translation services, more leaflets are needed in Turkish and in schools there are more students who do not speak German as a first language.
Other impacts	• The migrants who experience life in other countries return with new skills and knowledge, enriching the Turkish population.	• The increase in people promotes cultural diversity. • Germany currently has the lowest fertility rate in the EU, with only 1.36 children per woman. Migrants are usually young and will have children, which helps stabilise the birth rate.	• Many traditional Turkish people are concerned that the increased global attitude of their people is diluting the Turkish religious beliefs and cultural traditions.	• In the early 1990s a number of racial/ ethnic attacks on Turkish people fuelled concerns of social problems in Germany. • Many migrant workers who lived in Germany wanted citizenship but had to wait a very long time.

REVISION TIP

You may have studied a different case study than the one in this book. Take care not to get mixed up between the case studies, as this will cost you marks.

TEST YOUR REVISION

1. What is GIS?
2. What is the difference between immigration and emigration?
3. Describe how international migration has had an impact on the German economy.
4. Discuss how international migration from Turkey has had both a positive and negative impact on services.

Population Structure

A population pyramid is a graph that can be used to show the specific age breakdown of a population. It allows us to assess the different aspects of population structure and shows us what is happening to the birth rate, death rate and life expectancy of people in a particular country.

A MEDC population pyramid will have a much higher number of older people (at the top of the pyramid), even sides and a narrow base, whereas a LEDC pyramid will have a higher number of younger people (wide base of the pyramid), decreasing sides and a narrow top (with few people reaching old age).

Compare and contrast the structures of LEDCs and MEDCs

STAGE	POPULATION SHAPE	SHAPE DESCRIPTION	KEY INFORMATION
1 (LEDC)	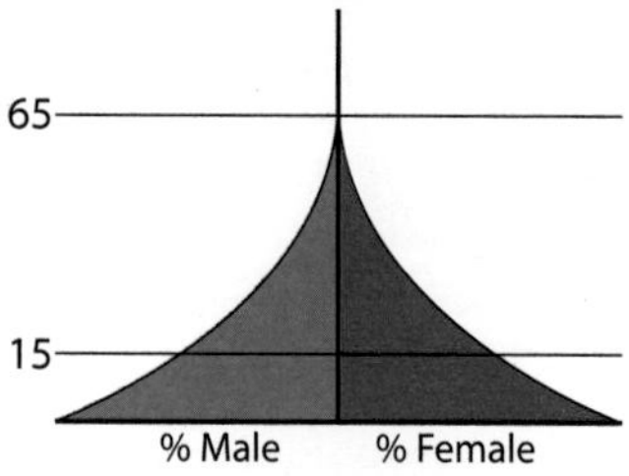 65 15 % Male % Female	**Concave**	High birth rate (<15). High death rate (15+) with a decreasing number of people in each age cohort. Very short life expectancy (around 30 years).
2 (LEDC)	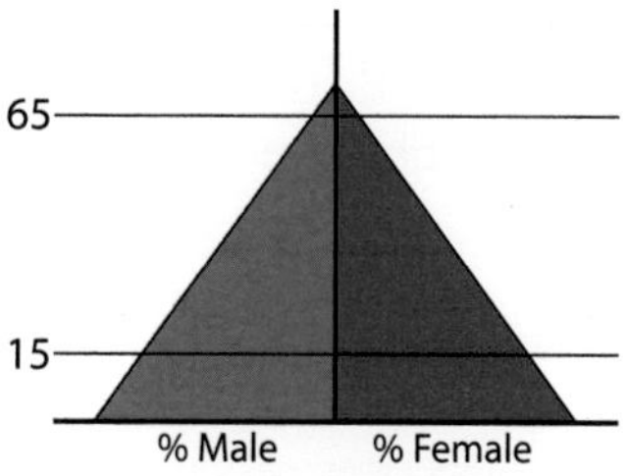 65 15 % Male % Female	**Triangle**	High birth rate (<15). Fall in death rate (15+) and slight increase in the number of people surviving in each age cohort. Still a short life expectancy (around 40 years).
3 (LEDC/ MEDC)	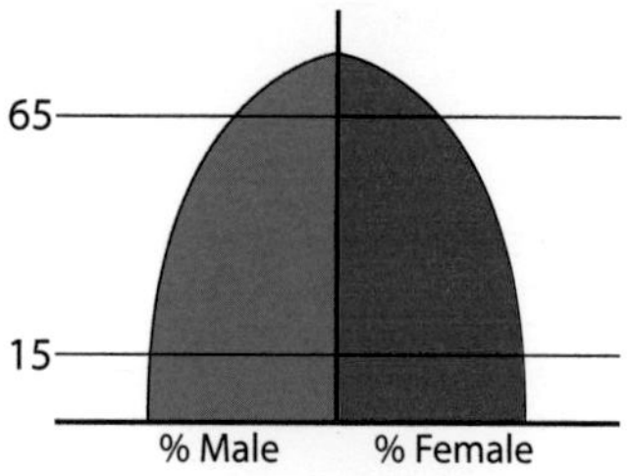 65 15 % Male % Female	**Tongue**	Falling birth rate (<15). Falling death rate (15–65). Life expectancy increases with more people living beyond 65.
4 (MEDC)	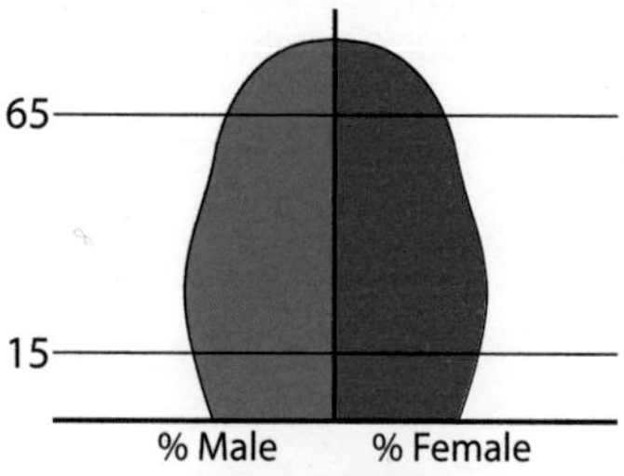 65 15 % Male % Female	**Leaf**	Low birth rate (<15). Low death rate (15–65). Life expectancy continues to increase with a high number of people living beyond 65. Average life expectancy reaches 75.
5 (MEDC)	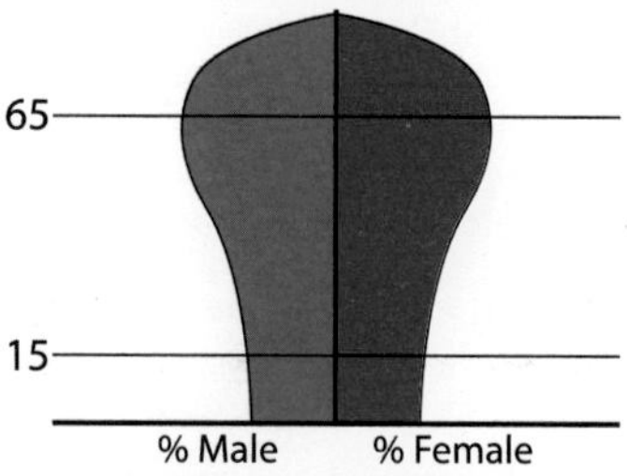 65 15 % Male % Female	**Hot air balloon**	Very low birth rate (<15). Low death rate (15–65). Life expectancy continues to increase and average life expectancy pushes up to 85 and beyond. Population structure is very 'top heavy'.

The social and economic implications of aged and youth dependency

A MEDC pyramid for an aged dependent population (the UK)

Population pyramid for the UK (MEDC) in 2010

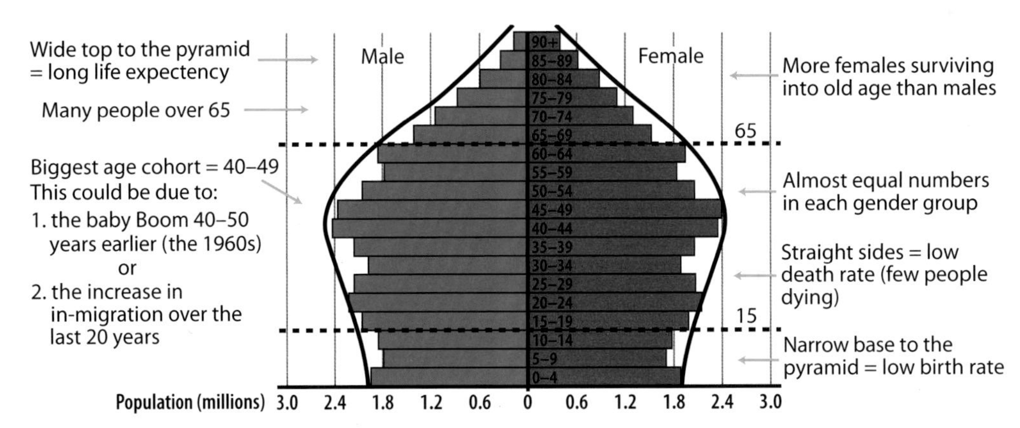

Data from U.S. Census Bureau, Public Information Office (PIO)

This is a population pyramid for the UK in 2010. It has steep sides as very few people are dying (death rate = 8/1,000) and the majority of children that are born (birth rate = 12/1,000) are surviving until they are 65 years old, if not older. This extended life expectancy is due to good health services. The UK could therefore be described as having an 'ageing' population, with a sizeable proportion of its population retired and older than 65.

The social and economic implications of an aged dependency

In MEDCs death rates have fallen due to improvements in:

- hygiene standards, sanitation, water and sewage treatment, and health education.
- medicine, resulting in cures, immunisation and vaccines.
- access to hospitals and doctors.
- diet and access to food supply.

As the population continues to get older, MEDCs often experience a range of social and economic issues that need to be addressed by the government.

SOCIAL IMPLICATIONS

1. Care for the elderly: As people get older they might find it difficult to look after themselves. Some might need support from a care worker. Others might have to move into sheltered accommodation or residential homes.

2. Impact on family life: As older family members are living longer this could mean that 65 year old children have to care for 90 year old parents. Families might have to make difficult decisions about how to best care for elderly relatives.

3. Medical issues: As medical care improves, people are living longer and suffer from 'degenerative' or long term illnesses (such as Alzheimer's or Parkinson's disease).

ECONOMIC IMPLICATIONS

1. Residential care: The government needs to spend an increased amount of money on the residential care of elderly people. As people live longer, there is a greater requirement for ground floor accommodation, lifts, single storey houses and sheltered accommodation.

2. Health Care: Quality healthcare for elderly people can be expensive and the government will need to spend an increased amount of money to cover prescriptions, dental treatment, home visits and home help.

3. Benefits: Each elderly person receives a state pension. Thirty years ago the average person would claim a pension for 7 years but today this is extended to at least 17 years. Pensions are therefore much more expensive and other benefits, such as free public transport, TV licences and winter fuel allowances, add to an increased financial burden.

A LEDC pyramid for a youth dependent population (Kenya)

Population pyramid for Kenya (LEDC) in 2010

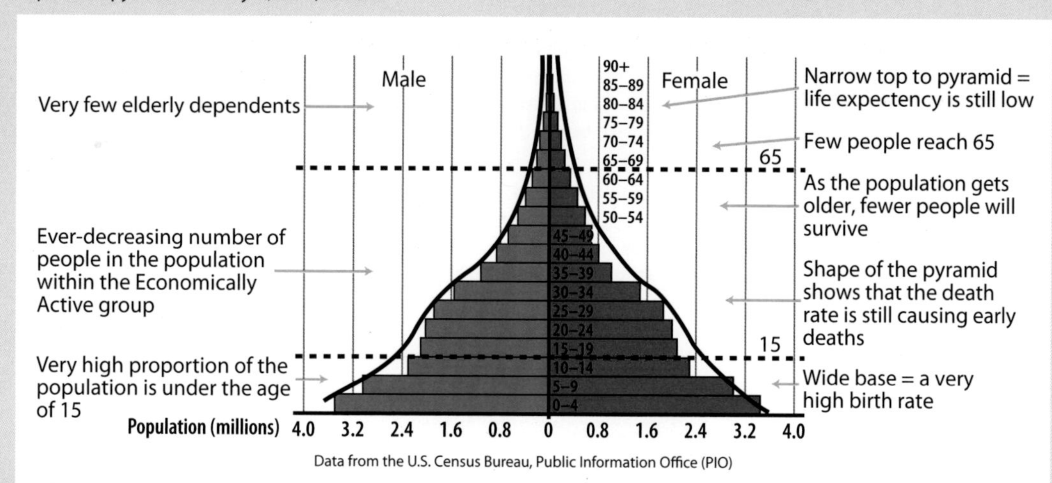

Data from the U.S. Census Bureau, Public Information Office (PIO)

This is a population pyramid for Kenya in 2010. It has a pronounced concave pyramid shape where the number of people in each age cohort continues to get smaller as the population gets older. Birth rates remain high (birth rate = 35/1,000) but death rates have plummeted in recent years (death rate = 8/1,000). The wide base of the pyramid indicates the high birth rate (and a total fertility rate of 4.4). However, the infant mortality rate in Kenya remains relatively high (about 47 for every 1,000 live births).

The social and economic implications of a youthful dependency

In LEDCs birth rates are high due to the following:

- The infant mortality and child mortality rates in most LEDCs remain high. Parents tend to have larger families to ensure that some survive.
- Many people in LEDCs are subsistence farmers. They need children to help provide a good supply of labour and to ensure that someone is available to care for them when they grow old.
- In LEDCs people do not have the same access to education. Often they do not know how to use family planning measures and many cannot afford them.

As more people are born and the population increases, LEDCs often face a range of social and economic issues due to the youthful nature of their population.

SOCIAL IMPLICATIONS		
1. Care for young people: Many young people have been made orphans by the death of their parents due to HIV/AIDS, Malaria or Tuberculosis. Orphanages are needed for these children.	**2. Medical issues:** Few doctors/hospitals result in people dying from basic illnesses. People cannot afford medicine or healthcare.	**3. Opportunities/education:** Few children in LEDCs have the opportunity of an education. This prevents them from gaining the skills to get 'formal' jobs, which would allow them to improve their living conditions.
ECONOMIC IMPLICATIONS		
1. Education: Many LEDCs are struggling to educate the population and the limited resources for schools and universities are being stretched even further.	**2. Healthcare**: Many people cannot afford even the most basic healthcare and they rely on patchy government support or aid agencies. Medicines are basic and can be expensive.	**3. Opportunities:** There is a lack of jobs and opportunities for people in LEDCs. A massive increase in the population means that there are more people now competing for the few jobs there are.

TEST YOUR REVISION

1. Describe the shape of a population structure showing an aged dependency.
2. Describe and explain the differences between LEDC and MEDC population structures.
3. Explain two economic implications of an aged population dependency.
4. Describe and explain two social implications of a youthful population dependency.

PART

SETTLEMENT SITE, FUNCTION AND HIERARCHY

The site and location of a settlement

Settlement: is a place where people live and work. It can be as large as a megacity or can be as small as individual houses dispersed in a farming area.

Site: is the exact place where a city, town or village might be located. Historically, this location was often chosen for its physical advantages, which were important when the site was first established.

Wet Point site: Settlers (the people choosing a site for settlement) need a clean drinking supply that is easy to reach. This constant water supply might also be used as a power supply.

Bridging point: 400 years ago, physical barriers such as deep or wide rivers provided a real challenge for settlers. Over time different methods were used to improve access and eventually bridges made rivers easy to cross.

Defensive site: Sometimes settlers would need protection against other tribes or families. A place on a hill or rock would give good views all around and a place built inside a river meander also meant that attack could only come from one easily defended access point.

Location/situation: is where the settlement is positioned with reference to what surrounds it. These surroundings include its physical features, its communication links and its neighbouring settlement.

Settlement hierarchy

Settlement hierarchy is used to rank the importance of places within a particular area. It is represented as a pyramid, with the most important settlement at the top and the least important at the base.

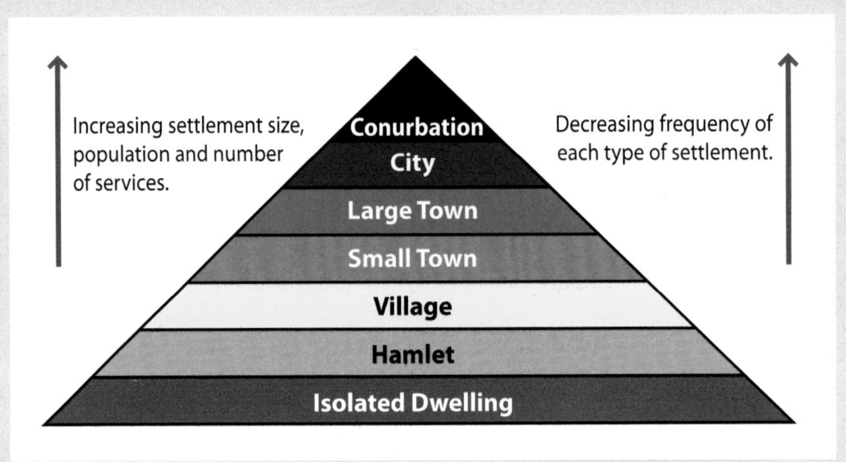

Settlement hierarchy

1. Population Size

The main way to decide the importance of a settlement is to count the number of people who live there.

CATEGORY	POPULATION
Conurbation	More than 1 million people
City	100,000 to 1 million people
Large Town	Less than 100,000 people
Small Town	Less than 20,000 people
Village	Less than 2,000 people
Hamlet	Less than 100 people
Isolated Dwelling	2–4 people

2. Function, high and low order

A function is the main activity/role of a settlement, and the economic and social development of a settlement area. The following are some of the main functions of a settlement:

- **Market town:** Where farmers buy and sell goods and services.
- **Mining town:** Where fuel and minerals are extracted.
- **Industrial town:** Where raw materials are processed into manufactured goods.

- **Port:** A transport hub for ships on the coast, a river or a lake.
- **Route centre:** Where settlement is located on junctions of several roads.
- **Service centre:** Where the area's specific needs and services are provided for.
- **Cultural/religious settlement:** Where people from other parts of the world come to live and study.
- **Administrative centres:** Where government offices and general office buildings are located.
- **Residential town:** Where people live but generally work elsewhere.
- **Tourist resort:** Where people visit to enjoy themselves and their recreational needs are catered for.

The goods and services in a settlement can be divided into high and low order. People are happy to travel long distances to purchase or use high order goods and services, such as buying a car or going on holiday. Low order goods and services are the things people want access to close to where they live, such as buying milk and newspapers.

3. Range

Range is the maximum distance that people will be prepared to travel to obtain a service. People are more likely to travel further for high order goods or services than for low order ones. The higher the number and complexity of the goods and services that a place provides, the further that people will travel to reach it.

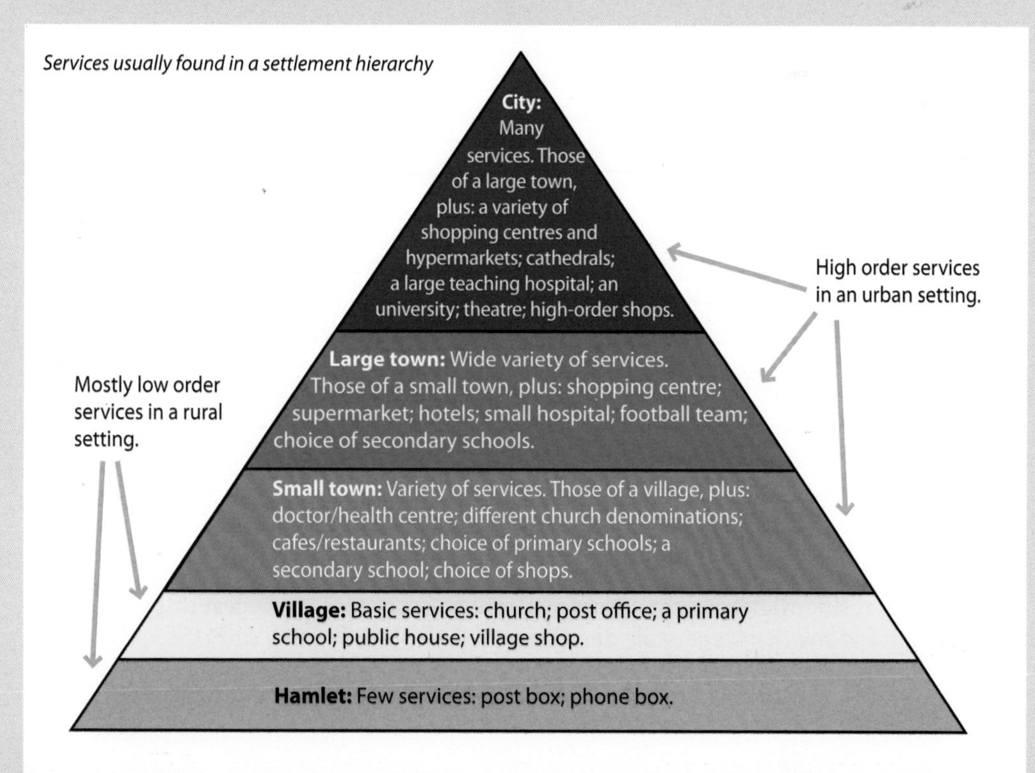

Sphere of influence (or market area) is the area that is served by a particular place. This area depends on the size and services of a town and the level of competition from rival settlements.

4. Threshold

Threshold is the number of people that are needed to ensure that there is enough demand for a particular service.

REVISION TIP

You need to know all four of the measures of settlement hierarchy in this section – make sure that you learn the definitions carefully so that you can apply them to both short and long questions.

TEST YOUR REVISION

1. What is a settlement?
2. Describe the difference between the site and location of a settlement.
3. Describe the reasons why settlers might want to set up their settlement at a defensive site.
4. How can range be used to measure settlement hierarchy?
5. How can function be used to determine settlement hierarchy?

The characteristics and location of land-use zones in MEDC cities

Land-use can change in different sectors of the city from the central business district (CBD), through the inner city, industrial zones, suburban residential area and to the rural-urban fringe.

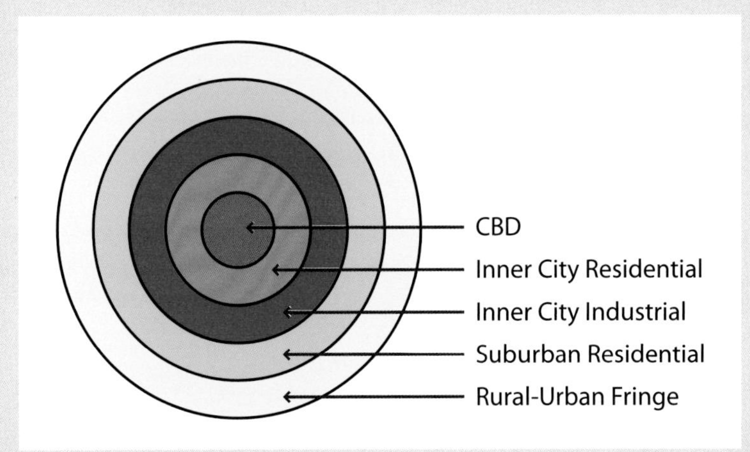

Typical shape for land-use zones in a MEDC city

Central Business District (CBD): is the core of the city's business and civic life. It is the place where business and retail are located, containing the main commercial streets and public buildings. Peak land values occur at the centre, where there are department stores, supermarkets, headquarters and offices for companies with large turnovers and high profits.

Inner city residential: As factories grew up close to the edge of the city, so too did the number of houses that were needed for workers. People could not afford transport costs so they needed to live within walking distance of their place of work.

Inner city industrial zone: Most old cities in the UK grew up because of heavy industries near the CBD. The inner city was the main source of income for UK cities in the nineteenth and twentieth centuries, as many people migrated into cities to work in new factories.

Suburban residential (suburbs): Residential areas account for the largest single use of land area in any city. Large-scale development took place in many cities throughout the twentieth century. It was fuelled initially by an increase in car ownership and public transport, as people no longer needed to live within walking distance of their work.

Rural-urban fringe: From the 1960s, many people had an increased disposable income and wanted more from where they lived. Urban sprawl took place with green field land turning into urban developments for private developments or outer-city council housing estates.

TEST YOUR REVISION

1. Describe the main characteristics of the Central Business District.
2. Explain why the inner city residential and industrial areas of the city were important for the growth of the city.
3. Why has the rural-urban fringe grown in recent years?

URBANISATION IN LEDCS AND MEDCS

The causes of urbanisation

PART 3

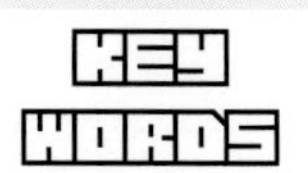

Urbanisation: is an increase in the proportion of people living in towns and cities, which usually takes place as a result of rural-urban migration.

Urban sprawl: is the process where green field land is turned into urban land on the rural-urban fringe.

Push and pull factors

Rural 'push' factors

Many people feel forced out of the countryside because:

- mechanisation means that there is less need for labour on the farms.
- people are starving, either due to too little output from the farm or crop failure and drought.
- there are few employment opportunities.
- there is overpopulation, resulting in high birth rates.
- there is pressure on the land (due to subdivision in families).

Urban 'pull' factors

Many people are attracted to cities because:

- they are looking for better paid jobs.
- they want better housing and a higher standard of living.
- there are more reliable food supplies.
- they want access to better services (such as schools and hospitals).
- religious and political activities can be carried out more safely in larger cities.

KEY WORDS

Counter Urbanisation: In many MEDCs the urban areas have reached their capacity in relation to urbanisation and some people have started to move back into the countryside from the urban areas.

The location, growth and characteristics of shanty towns

Case Study: Sao Paulo (a LEDC city)

The location of Sao Paulo

Location: South East Brazil, 30 miles from the Atlantic Ocean

Population: An estimated 20 million people in the wider metropolitan area

Shanty Towns: LEDC cities that have grown quickly often contain unplanned areas with poor quality housing and poor services, including access to clean water, electricity and sanitation.

Causes of urbanisation

A rapid increase in population	Pull factors that brought people to Sao Paulo	Push factors that moved people out of rural areas
• Large numbers of migrants moving from the poor, agricultural north east regions of Brazil to Sao Paulo. • A lot of international migration as many people from Portugal, Italy and Germany made their way to Sao Paulo. • High natural increase due to high birth rates and a lowering of the death rate.	• Good employment opportunities, with 50% of all Brazilian industry in Sao Paulo (construction, manufacturing and mining). • Good transport links (roads and railways) made it easier to migrate into the city.	• Farming was poorly paid and hard work. The perception was that work in the city was easier and better. • Rural areas have poor services compared to the big city. • Famines and drought put a strain on life in rural areas.

Characteristics of the Sao Paulo shanty towns (favelas)

A favela is a 'spontaneous' settlement. The local councils in Sao Paulo define it as being "an illegal occupation of terrain in a city where dwellers often have to live without basic infrastructure, such as waste, sewage, electricity, garbage collection, mail, etc."

Location

- As migrants arrive in Sao Paulo, many move to the informal favela settlements and build makeshift homes, constructed out of whatever materials they can find.
- The favelas are mostly built on wasteland, marshy land, land that is likely to flood or very hilly slopes, where no other building would be possible. They are usually near transport links, rivers and rubbish dumps.
- Many of the bigger favelas in Sao Paulo are located on the outskirts of the city. The biggest is called Heliopolis and is found in the south west area of the city. The second biggest, Paraisopolis (Paradise city) is located further away to the south and has a population of around 100,000 people.

Growth

- The rapid increase of the population of Sao Paulo is estimated at 2,000 new migrants arriving into the city each week.
- Favelas have been growing at a fast rate – by an estimated 120.6% from 1980–1990 and 57.9% from 1991–2000.

Key characteristics of the shanty towns (favelas)

Transport and Traffic
There is a huge dependence on the public transport system and it is struggling to cope. Congestion and traffic jams are common and there is much noise and air pollution.

Segregation
There is a very big divide between the rich and poor, and little social interaction between the different groups.

Housing
Poor residents live in permanent but poor quality housing between the inner city and the suburban favela, or in the very poor conditions of the favelas. One third of the population of Sao Paulo is estimated to live in one roomed dwellings.

Services
Basic services are limited in the favelas, with access to electricity, clean water, schools and doctors sporadic. Sewage often contaminates the water supply leading to health issues and disease, such as typhoid and dysentery.

Pollution
An industrial haze, intensified by traffic fumes, often hangs over the city. The city produces large amounts of waste which, in the favelas, is unlikely to be collected. Its presence, combined with polluted water supplies and sewage in open drains, can cause further health hazards.

Employment
There are not enough jobs and people are forced to work in the informal sector, where they provide basic services for a basic fee, eg roadside fruit selling, cutting hair, shoe shining and collecting rubbish.

Crime
The favelas are perceived as containing a lot of organised crime, violence and drug-trafficking.

TEST YOUR REVISION

1. Explain two push factors that might encourage people to move into the city.
2. Explain two pull factors that have encouraged the growth of shanty towns.
3. Describe the location of the shanty towns (favelas) in Sao Paulo.
4. Describe and explain some of the main characteristics of the Sao Paulo shanty towns.

Urban planning and regeneration of the inner city

Redevelopment: is when an area is demolished and redesigned. For example, in the inner city a street of terraced houses might be knocked down and replaced with a block of flats or other cheaper housing.

Regeneration: happens when an area is being upgraded. The aim is to improve the social and economic look of a place. It usually happens in an area where there is dereliction, pollution or out migration. It might allow some buildings to be restored.

Gentrification: is when an area is demolished and redesigned. However, the aim is that the original residents will not move back into the area. Instead, it aims to attract different, richer people, by building new, more expensive accommodation.

Urban Planning: is a very important aspect and initiator of change in urban environments. Planning allows any changes to occur in an organised, methodical manner that will add value to the place or area.

CASE STUDY

Case Study: Inner city Belfast (a MEDC city)

Belfast is a good example of a city that has had to deal with particular issues in poor, old areas of inner city.

1. The Laganside development began in 1989 with the building of the Lagan Weir (at a cost of £14 million), which would control the amount of water in the river and keep the mudflats covered at all times.
2. Much of Belfast's traditional manufacturing had grown up in Queen's Island but the decline of Harland and Wolff from over 20,000 workers to 500 in 2002 meant that there was around 185 acres of land that was not being used to its full potential.

Development of a strategy for Belfast Harbour area

Building began in 2006 with the aim to reinvent the old industrial brownfield site as the Titanic Quarter:

Housing
The 5,000 dwellings in Titanic Quarter should provide residential accommodation for about 20,000 people.

Transport
The BMAP (Belfast Metropolitan Area Plan) had plans to improve transport links in the area – especially in relation to the public transport networks. New bus services, walkways, bridges and cycle routes were developed in order to reduce congestion and air pollution across the city.

Image courtesy of Titanic Quarter Limited

Environment
- In the building of the Titanic Quarter, any industrial pollutants had to be removed from the site.
- A process of soil remediation was carried out where land contaminated by the shipbuilding industry was restored.
- Visually, the area has also been much improved.

Employment
- The £7 billion development is expected to create 25,000 jobs over the next 15 years. Initially these were construction but now include IT and financial services (Microsoft, Google, NI Science Park and Citibank/Citigroup), hotels (Premier Inn), museums, car show rooms (Audi) and the film industry (in the old Harland and Wolff Paint Hall).
- The types of job that the Titanic Quarter is bringing to the city are very different to the old heavy manufacturing that used to be on the same site. These jobs require new skills, new qualifications and more employees, which should help improve the diversity of the city.

Evaluate the sustainability of this urban planning scheme

A sustainable settlement is one which meets the needs of the present without compromising the ability of future generations to meet their own needs.

A sustainable city should aim to:

- manage resources, such as oil and forests, as effectively as possible.
- increase opportunities for recycling and reusing materials.
- ensure that the city grows in ways that minimise damage to wildlife and the countryside.
- source more resources, such as food, from the local area.

Planners can help to influence the sustainability of a city. Titanic Quarter has some of the following characteristics:

Society and people	Economic	Environmental
• The apartments built in Titanic Quarter provide more housing units than individual houses, giving the development a smaller 'urban footprint'. Generally, compact housing reduces heating bills and allows services such as access to water and bin collections to be shared. • Modern construction is designed to provide a light and attractive environment. People are encouraged to take pride in their areas, developing a sense of community and safety in the urban landscape.	• Long term employment opportunities are available in the local area. • The BMAP incorporates both social and gentrified housing schemes, allowing people with various incomes to live in the areas close to their employment.	• The Belfast harbour area was previously used for industry and its regeneration removes much of the old waste and pollution. • It is more sustainable to reuse this land than to develop greenfield sites at the edge of the city. • The developers of Titanic Quarter are committed to the reduction of waste and the recycling of waste materials.

TEST YOUR REVISION

1. What does the term 'urban planning' mean?
2. Describe some of the ways that Belfast has attempted to regenerate in recent years.
3. Evaluate the sustainability of an urban planning scheme that you have studied with reference to economic and environmental issues.

2B CONTRASTS IN WORLD DEVELOPMENT

THE DEVELOPMENT GAP

Identify the differences in development between MEDCs and LEDCs using social and economic indicators

Development: looks at the quality of life for humans within a country or area. It is linked to the economic wealth or progress that is experienced within that country and considers how foreign aid, political decisions, healthcare, education, poverty, infrastructure, human rights and the environment all work together to provide a particular quality of life.

The development gap: is the difference in economic activity, wealth and social measures between the rich MEDCs and poorer LEDCs. There is a large and widening difference between the quality of life experienced by a person living in a MEDC compared with that of someone living in a LEDC.

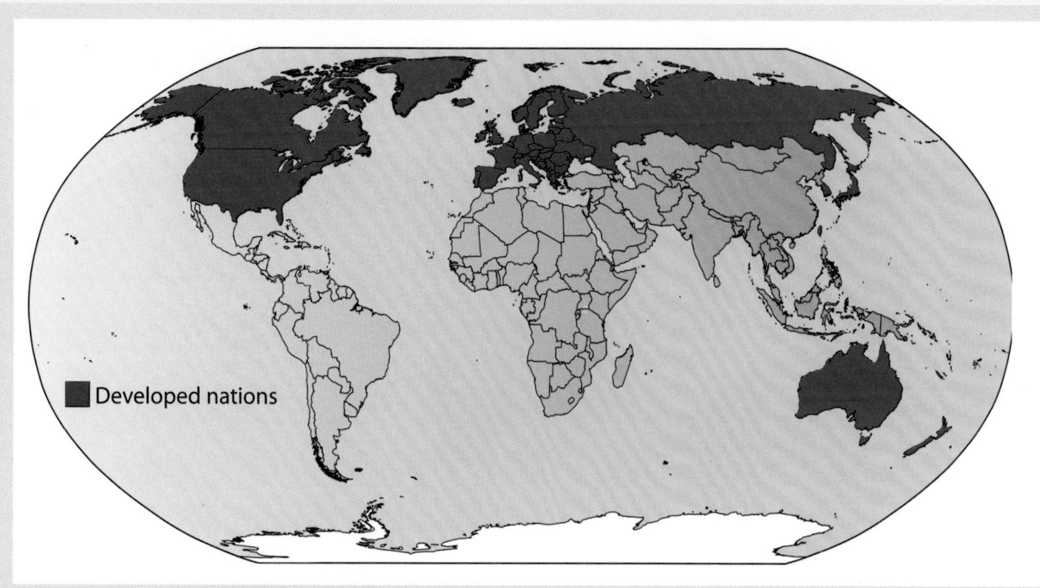

The north and south divide (MEDCs and LEDCs)

The indicators used to measure development

SOCIAL INDICATORS

1. Health

- ***Life expectancy*** shows the average lifespan of someone born in that country. The higher the life expectancy, the more developed the country is (eg UK = 78 years and Uganda = 41 years).
- ***The number of patients per doctor*** shows the inequality in healthcare provision between north and south. People in LEDCs have less access to doctors (eg Zambia = 1 doctor per 15,200 patients) than people in MEDCs (eg UK = 1 doctor per 360 patients).

2. Education

Adult Literacy Rate shows the percentage of the adult population who are able to both read and write. In the UK and other MEDCs you would expect this to be 99%, however, in Somalia (a LEDC) only 24% of adults can read and write.

ECONOMIC INDICATORS

1. Gross National Product (per capita) or Gross National Income

GNP shows the total economic value of all of the goods and services that are provided in a country during the course of a year, divided by the number of people who live in the country. The amount is always worked out in US Dollars so that a comparison can be made with other countries. The higher the GNP, the more developed a country will be. Increasingly GNP is being replaced with the term GNI (Gross National Income).

A MEDC is a More Economically Developed Country: This label usually refers to a country where the people tend to be relatively wealthy.

A LEDC is a Less Economically Developed Country: This label usually refers to a country where the people tend to be relatively poor.

Social indicators: are used to assess how well a country is developing in areas that affect its people such as health, education and diet.

Economic indicators: are used to show the amount of money or wealth within a country and how the people actually earn that wealth.

Newly Industrialised Countries (NICs): is a relatively new category used to describe countries who have not reached MEDC status but who are out-developing their fellow LEDCs. Currently South Africa, Mexico, Brazil, China, India, Malaysia, the Philippines, Thailand and Turkey are all listed as NICs.

ECONOMIC INDICATORS...

2. Percentage of people employed in primary activities

The percentage breakdown of jobs within each of the employment sectors can indicate development. A rich, more developed country is likely to have:

- more people working in the secondary, tertiary and quaternary sectors.
- a low number of people working in primary activities such as agriculture.

1. Primary activities are those jobs or economic activities where people are involved with collecting and working with raw materials or resources (eg farming/agriculture, mining, quarrying and fishing).

2. Secondary activities are those jobs where people are involved in manufacturing or making something (eg iron, bread and fizzy drinks) using the raw materials collected in the primary industry.

3. Tertiary activities are those jobs where people provide a service to others, (eg doctors, lawyers, teachers and hairdressers).

4. Quaternary activities are when people are involved in the research and development of new products. They mostly feature in the information technology industries.

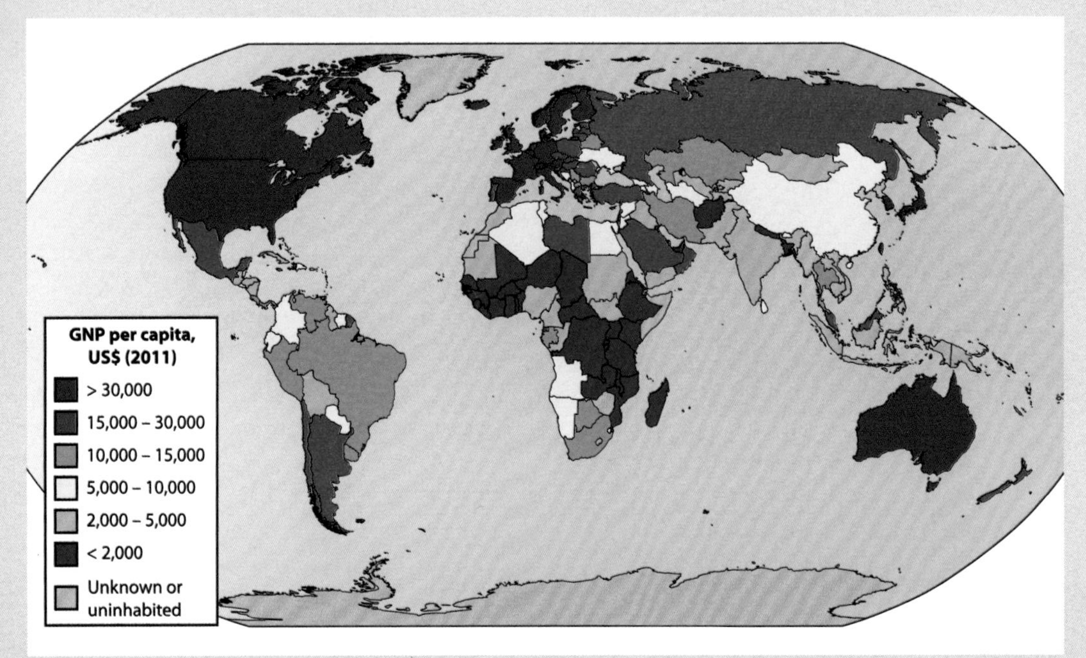

Using Gross National Product Per Capita to measure wealth across the world

Data from World Bank

COUNTRY	RANK	GNI $	COUNTRY	RANK	GNI $
Qatar	1	87,030	Niger	181	720
Luxembourg	2	64,410	Burundi	182	610
Norway	3	62,970	Eritrea	183	580
Singapore	4	59,790	Liberia	184	520
Switzerland	5	52,320	Congo (DR)	185	350

The five richest and five poorest countries as measured by GNI, 2011

Data from World Bank, International Comparison Program database, 2011

Assess the effectiveness of social and economic indicators of development in relation to quality of life using the Human Development Index (HDI)

The Human Development Index (HDI) is a composite measure, which combines measures in life expectancy, educational attainment and income. The HDI sets a minimum and maximum value for each dimension, called goalposts. It then shows where each country stands in relation to these goalposts as a value between 0 and 1, with 0 indicating minimum development and 1 maximum development.

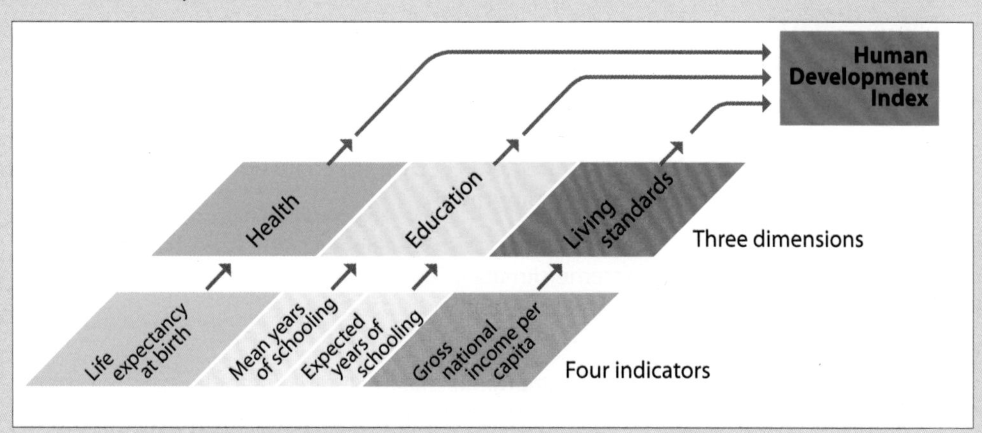

Components of the Human Development Index

Source: 2013 Human Development Index, United Nations Development Programme, http://hdr.undp.org/en/statistics/hdi/

Originally the three measures were life expectancy, adult literacy rates and GNP per capita. However, the education component of the HDI is now measured by the mean years of schooling for adults aged 25 years and expected years of schooling for children of school going age.

COUNTRY IN RANK ORDER	HUMAN DEVELOPMENT INDEX (HDI) VALUE	LIFE EXPECTANCY (YEARS)	MEAN YEARS OF SCHOOLING (YEARS)	EXPECTED YEARS OF SCHOOLING (YEARS)	GNI PER CAPITA ($PPP)
1 Norway	0.943	81.1	12.6	17.3	47,557
2 Australia	0.929	81.9	12.0	18.0	34,431
3 Netherlands	0.910	80.7	11.6	16.8	36,402
4 United States	0.910	78.5	12.4	16.0	43,017
5 New Zealand	0.908	80.7	12.5	18.0	23,737
183 Chad	0.328	49.6	1.5	7.2	1,105
184 Mozambique	0.322	50.2	1.2	9.2	898
185 Burundi	0.316	50.4	2.7	10.5	368
186 Niger	0.295	54.7	1.4	4.9	641
187 Congo, Democratic Republic	0.286	48.4	3.5	8.2	280

Top and bottom 5 Countries (Very High and Low Human Development, 2011)

Data from World Bank, International Comparison Program database, 2011

REVISION TIP

It is very easy to get confused when talking about the various measures of development. Make sure that you are clear about which are social, economic and composite measures of development.

TEST YOUR REVISION

1. What is the 'development gap'?
2. Identify one social indicator and explain how it measures differences in development.
3. Identify one economic indicator and explain how it measures differences in development.
4. Describe how the Human Development Index (HDI) measures development.
5. Evaluate the effectiveness of the Human Development Index (HDI) in measuring development.

The factors that hinder development in LEDCs

1. Historical Factors
Colonial history has had an important impact on the development of many places across the world. Being part of a European Empire brought advantages (eg trade) but also many disadvantages. The rulers could force their subjects to fight in their armies, tax them and take their main assets (eg mineral wealth and land).

2. Environmental Factors
Environmental issues can cause people who are already poor to struggle further and put them at greater risk than people who live in MEDCs:

a. ***Natural Hazards***
The impact of natural hazards is greater in LEDCs, which do not have money to either plan for hazards or cope with their aftermath.

b. ***Extreme Climates***
Many LEDCs experience extreme climates. The people find it difficult to grow their own food and there is much malnutrition and starvation.

c. ***Natural Resources***
Much of the farmland in LEDCs is marginal, making it difficult for farmers to produce a good crop. Water supplies can also be limited, making it difficult for people to survive.

3. Dependence on Primary Activities
Countries that have a source of mineral wealth (eg iron ore) or energy resources (eg coal, oil or natural gas) are more likely to develop industrially. This means that countries move from a dependence on primary activities (eg agriculture) to a dependence on secondary activities (eg manufacturing). Global trade systems ensure that raw materials are processed in MEDCs so that they can maximise the profit in the finished product. Some LEDCs find that a close dependence on primary products means that they can be pressurised into accepting lower prices for the unprocessed raw material. These prices can fluctuate significantly and are dependent on global markets.

4. Debt
Many LEDCs need investment in order to make improvements to infrastructure (eg transport links, hospitals and schools). As the countries cannot afford to raise the money themselves, they sometimes borrow money from other countries and international organisations. Any money borrowed must be paid back with interest and often takes a very long time to pay off. The money tied up in paying off debts cannot be used to fund further development projects.

5. Politics
Some LEDCs have unstable and corrupt governments, with a few people holding all of the power, money and influence. They become rich even though the majority of people remain very poor and aid does not reach the people who need it the most.

TEST YOUR REVISION

1. Explain how historical factors might hinder the development of a LEDC.
2. Explain the impact that environmental factors might have on development in a LEDC.
3. How can a dependence on primary activities be a negative influence within a LEDC?

Describe one named strategy that is attempting to reduce the global development gap and explain how it attempts to do so

The Jubilee Debt Campaign

JUBILEE DEBT CAMPAIGN

The Organisation

The Jubilee Debt Campaign (www.jubileedebt.org.uk) is a successor to Jubilee 2000, an organisation that sought debt cancellation to mark the beginning of a new millennium. It was set up to cancel debt owed by 52 of the world's poorest nations. Its petition of support had over 24 million signatures from over 166 nations. As of 2014, $130 billion of debt had been cancelled for 35 countries following the campaign.

The core aims of the strategy

The main aim of Jubilee 2000 was to attempt to get third world debt wiped out. However, many of the promises made by governments in 2000 were not honoured and the work of the Jubilee Debt Campaign continues so that they can:

1. Cancel unjust debts.
2. Make lenders act more responsibly to prevent new debt crises.

The action taken

1. ***Ending the Vulture Culture:*** A 'vulture fund' is when a private finance company buys up the debt of others. These companies often gain profit from the poverty of others by suing the country that has defaulted on debt obligations. The Jubilee Debt Campaign has supported campaigns to end this practice, including getting a law passed in the UK in 2010.
2. ***Cancelling debts of countries following crisis:*** The Jubilee Debt Campaign got extra debts cancelled for Haiti in 2010 following its devastating earthquake, and for Guinea, Liberia and Sierra Leone in 2015 after the Ebola outbreak.
3. ***No new debt crisis:*** There is currently a boom in lending to the most impoverished countries. The Jubilee Debt Campaign is calling for various measures to prevent this causing new debt crises, including making more 'aid' money grants rather than loans, measures to make lending more responsible, and a 'bankruptcy' process for governments so that banks no longer think they will be bailed out for reckless loans.

TEST YOUR REVISION

1. Describe the aims of one named strategy that is attempting to reduce the global development gap.
2. Explain the actions taken by one named strategy that is attempting to reduce the global development gap.

PART 2

FACTORS CONTRIBUTING TO UNEQUAL DEVELOPMENT

How does globalisation both help and hinder development? (with reference to one case study from a LEDC or NIC)

HOW GLOBALISATION HAS HELPED DEVELOPMENT?
1. Globalisation creates jobs in LEDCs, giving employees a reliable source of income in formal jobs.
2. Often MNCs will spend money to improve the social conditions and local infrastructure. Governments, keen to attract vital foreign investment, will spend money improving roads, airports and communication links.
3. Additional revenue means that foreign investment and money is coming into the economy.
4. People will learn and develop new skills, and often receive better education.
5. New skills, technology and specialist machinery will be brought into a poor country, making it more modern.

Globalisation: is the process of the world becoming more interconnected and interdependent. People around the world are more connected to each other than ever before, largely due to developments in transport, technology, communications and the Internet.

Multinational Companies (MNCs) are companies that manufacture goods in more than one country. Many of the biggest MNCs have offices and factories in every main country across the world. In recent years, the trend has been for MNCs to locate their factories in LEDCs. Here the labour costs are lower, allowing the companies to increase their profit.

HOW GLOBALISATION HAS HINDERED DEVELOPMENT?
1. Although jobs are created in LEDCs, the rate of pay tends to be much lower than in MEDCs.
2. Working conditions can be poor in LEDCs, with employees working long hours in an uncomfortable and sometimes unsafe environment.
3. In reality the depth of foreign investment is minimal. All profits flow back to the headquarters in the MEDC and the LEDC does not have the same access to the wealth.
4. There is no guaranteed job security. Many of the jobs in LEDCs are semi-skilled and easily replaced. If a country has chosen to relocate manufacturing once, there is nothing to stop them moving again to a country where more incentives are offered.

Case Study: A globalisation case study (from a LEDC or NIC) Nike™ and China

Company details:

- Founded Oregon, USA, 1964
- 700 shops worldwide
- Employs more than 800,000 workers in 600 contract factories in 46 countries.
- In the 1980s it decided to concentrate design and marketing in the USA and sub-contract production to factories in LEDCs.
- Has been working in China for 30 years, with over 272,000 workers in 170 factories.

The advantages to Nike of locating their factories in China:

- **Cheap labour:** Wages are low in China (sometimes as little as 50p per hour).
- **Cheap land and services:** Land for factories is less expensive than in the USA, as are electricity and transport costs.
- **Lower taxes:** The government has given incentives and charges lower taxes and rates to attract MNCs.
- **Fewer worker rights:** Employees are not allowed to join unions, take paid holidays or receive sick pay and can be made redundant much more easily than employees in a MEDC.

How globalisation has helped development in China

The advantages to China of Nike locating their factories in China:

- Investment by Nike helps the Chinese economy, brings better jobs and often a better standard of employment and living.
- Facilitating global companies such as Nike has led to improvements in the services and infrastructure within China, as global companies require global transport and communication links.
- Nike claims that it has been instrumental in improving working conditions for employees within China, enhancing regulations for fire safety, air quality, minimum wages and overtime limits.
- Nike locating its factories in China will attract other MNCs who are looking for new production bases.

How globalisation has hindered development in China

The disadvantages to China of MNCs locating their factories in China:

- Wages are still quite low on a global scale.
- Many of the jobs are low skilled and do not require high levels of education.
- Although working conditions are improving in some Chinese factories, most workers are still working and living in conditions that are much worse than the global norm.
- Much of the profits generated inevitably go to the headquarters in Europe or the USA and not to the factory in China.
- There is always the possibility that a MNC could pull out of China and take its jobs to another country that will give the company a better deal.

How does the pattern of world trade create problems for LEDCs?

There is no country in the world that is self-sufficient and able to produce its own raw materials, goods and services. Countries need each other. Interdependence is when a relationship is built up between countries to exchange goods and services.

The balance of trade

The balance of trade is the difference between the cost of imports and the value of exports.

Trade: is the flow and movement of goods and services between producers and consumers. Good trade links are essential for the development of any country.

Imports: refer to the products bought and brought into a country.

Exports: are the products sold and sent to another country.

World trade pattern

LEDCs make most of their money through the export of primary materials. The problem with this is that the LEDCs are highly susceptible to price changes on the raw materials.

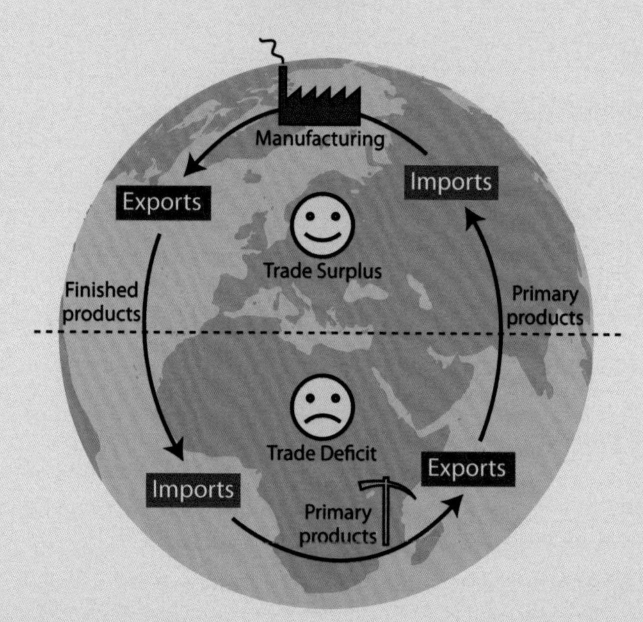

Trade issues for LEDCs

1. **Reliance on primary products:** LEDCs are reliant on the export of one or two primary products to help them generate foreign currency (eg 90% of Zambia's exports come from copper). It is very risky for a country to rely on one product, for example, a bad harvest could lead to loss of export earnings on agricultural products. Also, prices for primary products tend to fluctuate more than prices for secondary manufactured goods.
2. **Tariffs:** The customs duties that are attached to imports are called tariffs. Tariffs give an advantage to manufacturers of locally produced goods over similar goods that are imported. They also help raise revenues for governments.
3. **Trading blocs:** Most countries around the world are part of at least one trade bloc. This allows imports and exports to be made without incurring tariffs, encouraging 'free' trading and helping to protect the price of goods produced within the bloc (eg the UK and Spain are both members of the EU, which means that goods produced in Spain can be sold tariff-free in the UK and vice versa).

TEST YOUR REVISION

1. Describe how globalisation can be both a help and a hindrance to a LEDC.
2. What are Multinational Companies (MNCs)?
3. With reference to a case study from a LEDC, describe how globalisation has impacted development in one country.
4. Explain what is meant by the term 'balance of trade'.
5. What impact might tariffs have on development in LEDCs?

PART 3

SUSTAINABLE SOLUTIONS TO DEAL WITH THE PROBLEMS OF UNEQUAL DEVELOPMENT

A sustainable project that uses appropriate technology (in a LEDC)

The gap has been widening between MEDCs and LEDCs. Many want to ensure that this gap does not continue to widen and that new solutions are sought to allow LEDCs and NICs to progress and develop.

Any project that is defined as sustainable must:

- improve quality of life
- improve living standards
- encourage economic development
- give future generations a higher chance of survival
- not harm the environment
- use appropriate technology

Appropriate technology

Often in LEDCs, hi-tech solutions to problems are inappropriate for the inhabitants as they do not have easy access to energy sources or replacement parts. Appropriate technology will provide an innovation that is suitable for the local people.

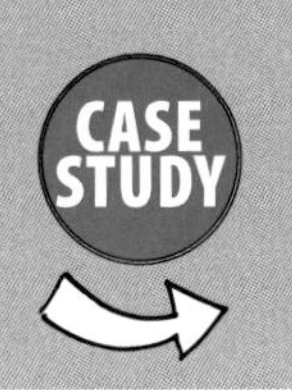

Case Study: The development of a borehole and hand pump in Uganda (a LEDC)

The problem

- Uganda's water quantity (amount) and quality (standard) is poor in places. Some families have to walk over a mile each way to fetch water. Few people have access to safe water and water-borne diseases are rife.
- Water-borne diseases are thought to cause around 2 million deaths worldwide every year. The UNHCR estimates that 1.1 billion people worldwide lack clean drinking water.

fields of life
CHANGING LIVES, BUILDING HOPE

Describe and explain the solution

- **Fields of Life** is a charity that has been working in Uganda since 1993.
- They help to supply safe, clean water – especially to vulnerable and marginalised groups.
- They have the capacity to drill 10 wells per month using their own drilling rigs. This provides clean water for 1,000 people. It is their vision to provide 1 million people with 1,000 wells over 10 years.

Why is this appropriate technology?

The initial investment into a village is made through donations to Fields of Life. This provides the necessary materials to complete the construction of a well, which currently costs £4,000 to drill. The technology that is left in each village is appropriate for the needs of the local people:

- **Cost:** They do not have to pay any money for the construction of the well but a local community committee is set up to collect small amounts of money for a maintenance fund.

KEY WORDS

Sustainable development: is "development that meets the needs of the present without compromising the ability of future generations to meet their own needs."

Appropriate Technology: is technology that is suited to the needs, skills, knowledge, resources and wealth of local people, in the environment in which they live.

- **Technology:** A hand pump is installed at each borehole rather than a mechanical pump (which is more complicated and might require more maintenance and moving parts).
- **Responsibility of upkeep:** Some local people are trained to fix simple problems with the well.
- **Community involvement and organisation:** The Fields of Life team prepare the local community in advance of digging any well to ensure that free access is granted to the water source.
- **Education and hygiene:** Fields of Life provide basic training about water use and sanitation. They educate on the safe storage of water and how to dig long drop toilets to ensure that drinking water and sewage do not mix.

Evaluate the success of the appropriate technology project

Economic improvements	Environmental improvements	Social improvements
1. **Time:** Children and women do not have to spend long periods of time looking for and carrying water for the family, which means that they have time to go to school, making them better educated, more employable and improving their future. 2. **Industry:** A regular supply of water allows villagers to engage in small business ventures like making tea for tourists or cooking and baking. 3. **Farming:** Water can be used for the irrigation of vegetable patches and drinking water for animals. 4. **Health benefits:** Clean water means that people suffer less from illness and disease. People will have more time and energy to work.	1. **Environmental impact:** Wells and boreholes do not cause damage to the environment as long as they are carefully positioned. 2. **Animals:** A source of water means that animals can be kept alive through drought conditions. 3. **Pollution:** Hand pumps do not produce pollution as they no not need energy. Often a pump encourages villagers to take care in looking after the physical environment of the area.	1. **Shared responsibility:** The well is left in the care of local villagers and they develop a new sense of shared responsibility to manage the well and to ensure that there are no pollutants leaking into the ground water. 2. **New community spirit:** The well often brings communities together with a new spirit and hope for a better life. 3. **Feeling better:** The water comes from deep underground which means that it is always clean. Less disease means that people feel better about life. 4. **Empowerment:** Women, in particular, are given an opportunity to claim back lost time and can use this time to earn money. Incidences of violence to women are reduced, as they do not have to travel back and forth to a clean water source.

Fairtrade and the advantages it brings to LEDCs

Why is Fairtrade good for producers?

1. **Fair and stable prices:** For Fairtrade products, buyers have to pay the Fairtrade minimum price. This price is good for producers as it aims to cover the costs of sustainable production and means that when the market price falls below a sustainable level, farmers do not lose out.
2. **Fairtrade for development:** Producers are also paid a Fairtrade premium, which is an extra amount paid beyond the price of the goods that the producer can spend on whatever they want.
3. **Empowering small-scale farmers:** Fairtrade was set up to help empower the small-scale farmer and improve their working conditions. In some products, such as coffee, cocoa and cotton, Fairtrade only certifies small farmer organisations. It also aims to protect the environment in a sustainable manner.

Fairtrade is a strategy used to provide an organised approach to help producers in LEDCs gain better trading conditions and promote sustainability. It gives workers who were previously under pressure from the usual trade practices to get a fair price for their efforts.

What is aid? Evaluate how aid brings both benefits and problems to LEDCs

Aid: is the process of one country or organisation giving resources to a country that needs help. The type of aid given depends on the circumstances and might include money, expertise (doctors, aid workers or rescue specialists) or goods (food, water, shelter or tools). The givers of aid tend to be in MEDCs and the recipients of aid tend to be in LEDCs.

Short term aid: is often in response to an emergency and is usually linked to a particular need, for example, the provision of food and water following a natural disaster.

Long term aid: is a more far-reaching and sustainable type of help which is given over a long period of time. Often it will take a long time for any impact to be noted.

When studying development, it can be easy to concentrate only on key words and definitions, so make sure that you know how to evaluate the positives and negatives of some of the issues (including aid and appropriate technology).

Bilateral, multilateral, voluntary and tied aid

Bilateral aid: is aid that is given directly from one government to another government. Bilateral means that two countries are involved and the aid is usually tied.

Multilateral aid: is aid that is given from national governments to world/international organisations such as the World Bank, the World Health Organisation or the United Nations. This money is then distributed to the various development projects that need it around the world.

Voluntary aid: is sometimes called 'charitable aid'. Many charities (NGOs: non-governmental organisations) are based in MEDCs and have a particular interest in a part of the world, medical issue or cause. They are usually funded by the public and organise their own aid programmes and projects on a small scale within countries.

Tied aid: is money given by a donor government that is specified for particular projects (eg a government might give £20 million to a country but specify that the money should be used for building hospitals, schools or roads). Often the donor country also benefits economically from the aid.

THE BENEFITS OF AID	THE PROBLEMS WITH AID
• Much short term and humanitarian aid can help to save lives following a natural disaster or war. • As short term aid is brought in as actual goods by charities, there is less chance of it being sold to pay for political corruption. • Aid can help to improve the standard of living of people in recipient countries and if used properly and focused effectively, it will allow a country to develop and improve in a sustainable manner.	• Aid does not always reach the poorest people who really need it. Political corruption and poor administration systems can mean that aid can fail to reach the people. • Many LEDCs have come to depend on the regular flow of aid. This means that if the flow ever ceases (eg during a global recession) it could cause problems for the people in the LEDC. • It can be difficult for countries to become independent if they rely on other countries for handouts. • Aid can undermine local producers. As new food supplies come into the country this can have a negative impact on the prices of produce grown and sold within the country, causing the local economy to decline.

TEST YOUR REVISION

1. What is 'appropriate technology'?
2. With reference to one sustainable project that uses appropriate technology, explain how economic and environmental improvements have occurred.
3. Explain two reasons why Fairtrade can be good for producers.
4. Describe the difference between bilateral and multilateral aid.
5. Explain two reasons why aid does not always bring benefits to people living in LEDCs.

2C MANAGING OUR RESOURCES

1. The Impact of Our Increasing Use of Resources on the Environment
2. Increasing Demand for Resources in LEDCs and MEDCs
3. Managing Waste to Protect our Environment
4. Sustainable Tourism to Preserve the Environment

THE IMPACT OF OUR INCREASING USE OF RESOURCES ON THE ENVIRONMENT

The human impact on the environment in terms of carbon footprints

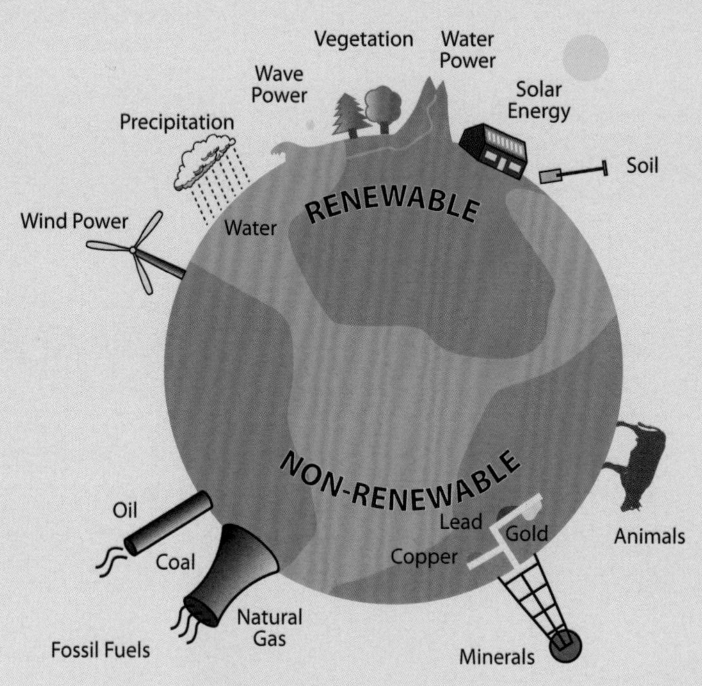

The main renewable and non-renewable resources for our planet

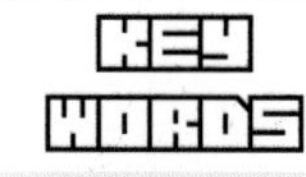

Resources: are substances obtained from the environment that help us to satisfy human needs. People need a wide variety of resources such as water to drink, air to breath, food for energy, heat, light and a cooking source.

A renewable resource: is one that is naturally replaced and can be used repeatedly.

A non-renewable/ finite resource: is one that can only be used once. It is usually burnt or manufactured into something else and therefore cannot be used again.

The global population is increasing at a very fast rate. This increase means that more people need to share the same amount of resources, and, as the majority of resources we use are non-renewable, they are going to run out faster. In addition, more people than ever before have a 'disposable' income that allows them to buy new electronic products, which further increase the demand for power supplies. 86% of global energy comes from non-renewable sources with 13% coming from renewables. In recent years we have started to suffer from the effects of resource depletion.

Carbon footprint: is the total set of greenhouse gas emissions that are caused by an organisation, event, product or person. It is usually measured by the amount of carbon dioxide and methane emissions within a population.

Resource depletion: is when some of the raw materials that we have come to depend on are running out and becoming exhausted.

The carbon footprint recognises that every action people take has an environmental consequence. As people use particular resources, they will produce greenhouse gases through the transportation, storage and presentation of products.

Why are the carbon footprints so high in MEDCs?

Higher car ownership: Most families have at least one car in MEDCs and many have more than one. Personal motorised transport is a major source of carbon dioxide in the atmosphere.

Large homes and modern appliances: It takes a lot of energy to heat, cool and power homes in MEDCs. People have more disposable income than those in LEDCs, giving them more money to spend on buying technology, which uses a lot of energy.

Transport: People in MEDCs travel greater distances than those in LEDCs, both within their country and on holiday from their country.

Food: Much of the food eaten in MEDCS is imported, eg tropical fruit, which has been flown many miles.

Identify and evaluate measures to manage traffic in a sustainable manner (using one case study of a city within the EU)

Case Study: Freiburg, Southern Germany

Location map of Freiburg

Sustainable measures used to manage traffic

Most cities with a population of 225,000 find that congestion, pollution and traffic jams are constant issues. Freiburg City Council has adopted a number of strategies to help solve these issues:

1. **Public transport:** Freiburg has an excellent public transport system operated by VAG Freiburg. There is an extensive network of electric trams across the city which are efficient, quick and cheap.
2. **Pedestrians encouraged:** Freiburg has an extensive pedestrian zone in the centre of the city where no cars are allowed.
3. **Cycling encouraged:** Over 400 miles of cycle paths have been created with bikes getting priority on roads and at traffic lights. Safe bike storage was introduced, with over 6,000 bike parking slots. Many people cycle everywhere and do not even own a car.
4. **Car use discouraged:** Many areas of the city are car-free. Free parking has been replaced with high car-parking charges. In the Vauban neighbourhood, residents have to sign an agreement that they will never own a car.

Evaluation of sustainability in Freiburg

Freiburg has organised its transport to make the integrated transport model sustainable. They have taken more measures to reduce the carbon footprint than any other German city.

POSITIVE IMPACTS OF SUSTAINABLE MEASURES	NEGATIVE IMPACTS OF SUSTAINABLE MEASURES
Fewer cars: It is easier to travel by bike or tram into the city. People are encouraged to avoid buying a car. Over the last 10 years carbon emissions have been reduced by 10%.	**Public transport links and times are limited:** Trams tend to be concentrated in the city centre and don't cover the urban rural fringe. The transport times do not suit people who work unsociable hours.
Greater use of public transport: 68% of trips in the city are made using the tram. The transport system is continually being integrated, with cycle racks at railway and tram stations.	**Overcrowded public transport:** At peak times the trams and buses can become overcrowded.
Reduced congestion: Congestion is reduced across the city, which means that there is less pollution.	**Problems for people with car dependent jobs:** Some people require cars for their jobs. It can also be difficult to get deliveries into shops in the city centre and to get larger purchases back home from the city.
Improved environment: Increased pedestrian areas make the city look and feel better, and green spaces have been improved to absorb carbon dioxide.	**Car ownership is still high:** Although car use has been reduced, many people still own and use cars regularly.

REVISION TIP

This case study is the first of four case studies in this unit. It is important that you learn each case study in detail and know the positive and negative impacts that support any answer when you are asked to evaluate.

TEST YOUR REVISION

1. What is a carbon footprint?
2. Explain two reasons why carbon footprints in MEDCs might be high.
3. What sustainable measures did Freiburg use to manage traffic efficiently?
4. Discuss two positive and two negative impacts of the sustainable measures of transport management in Freiburg.

INCREASING DEMAND FOR RESOURCES IN LEDCs AND MEDCs

Population growth

As the global population increases, pressure is put on global resources. There is a huge demand for the consumption of non-renewable energy and fossil fuel use continues to increase.

Economic developments in LEDCs

The demand for electricity is increasing in NICs and LEDCs. As LEDCs attempt to expand their economy by setting up factories to manufacture goods prior to export, their dependence on non-renewable resources also increases.

PRESSURE ON PEOPLE

Living space: Increasing population densities are forcing some people to live in slums or shanty towns. In China, 95% of the population live on 32% of the land, creating a high population density (364 people per km^2).

Food production: 54% of the land in India is used for arable farming, yet it continues to have difficulties in growing enough food for its expanding population.

Water: The UN Environment Programme highlights 10 areas across the continent of Africa where water will be under extreme stress by 2025 and estimates that this will affect nearly 600 million people. It identifies increasing population pressure and climate change as the two main factors which are driving this change.

Steel: The demand for iron and steel is caused by the building/ urbanisation programmes in LEDCs. China alone will use around 32 billion tonnes of iron over the next 10 years. This will push up the cost of living for people.

PRESSURE ON THE ENVIRONMENT

Land: LEDC cities are increasing all the time as people move from the countryside to urban areas. As these cities grow they take up more rural landscape and destroy natural environments and animal habitats.

Natural resources: Methods used to collect raw materials can cause environmental problems. Open cast mining, large scale tree-felling and gas extraction techniques (eg fracking) can all damage the natural environment.

Waste management: People today produce more waste than at any other time (around 200 kg of rubbish per person per year). Disposing of this waste by burning or landfill produces air pollution and smog.

Air pollution and global warming: As many LEDCs are investing in industry for the first time, there has been an increase in air pollution. The World Health Organisation estimates that over 750,000 people die every year from air pollution in China.

Evaluate the benefits and problems of one renewable energy source as a sustainable solution

Renewable energy: is a source of energy that comes from alternative sources (eg wind, solar and biofuels) where the mechanism for providing the energy can be used and repeated over and over.

Solar energy: is a renewable energy source which is created using the sun's energy to produce power. The sun's heat and light is converted into electricity using the energy of speeding photons within a solar panel.

Wind energy: is a renewable energy source that is created using the force of the wind to turn the sails on a turbine to generate power.

Biofuel: is a renewable energy source that can be created using fermented animal or plant waste. Power is generated as the biological materials rot and create chemical energy.

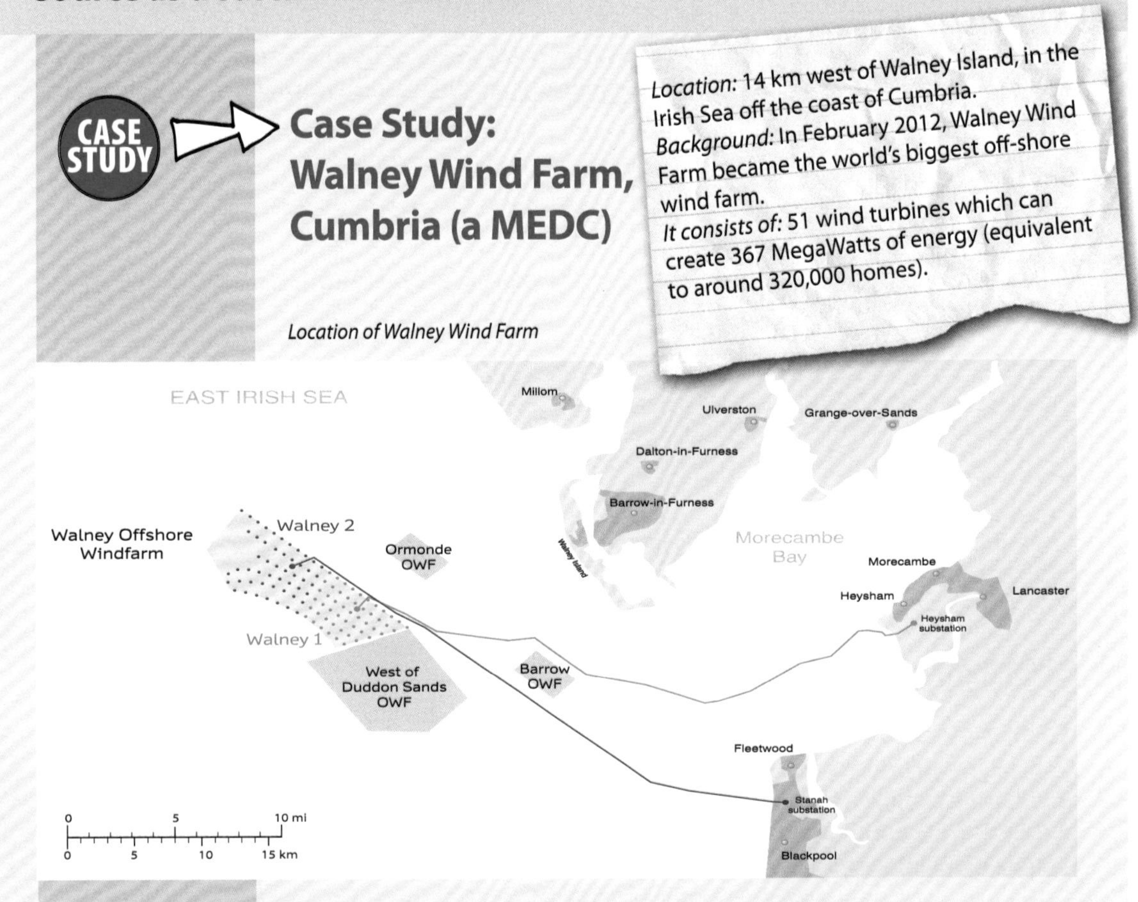

Location of Walney Wind Farm

BENEFITS OF DEVELOPING WIND POWER	PROBLEMS OF DEVELOPING WIND POWER
Reduced carbon emissions: Much of the UK's energy comes from fossil fuels that create greenhouse gases and carbon emissions. A move to a renewable source provides an inexhaustible, locally available, 'green' fuel.	**Harm to wildlife:** Some scientists have concerns that the electric field created by generators in the turbines might affect the sense of direction of seals, porpoises, sharks and whales.
Sustainable energy source: Wind power is cost-effective and modern wind turbines are reliable – lasting over 20 years. The UK also has access to the most reliable wind patterns in Europe. The UK aims to obtain 20% of its electricity from renewable sources by 2020.	**Visual pollution:** Some people find the wind farms ugly and feel that they will put tourists off coming to an area. However, the contractor argues that it is difficult to see the wind farm as it is 14 km offshore.
Reduced dependence on imported fossil fuels: The UK has become very dependent on fossil fuels, which are mostly imported from other countries. Any reduced dependence helps the UK with its energy security.	**The need for alternative sources of energy:** On calm or very windy (above 16 knots) days the turbines cannot be used. This means that a backup energy system is always needed (a non-renewable power station which can be brought to full capacity quickly).
Value for money: Wind power can be expensive but as fossil fuels become more expensive to use wind power is starting to be seen as a better long term solution.	**High set up costs:** The initial investment of £1 billion is seen as being very expensive. However, the turbines require minimal maintenance and guarantee a fixed income for a minimum of 20 years.

REVISION TIP

Sometimes trying to learn lots of facts about the different case studies can get confusing. Try using a separate page to write up each case study.

TEST YOUR REVISION

1. What are the two main reasons why there is an increased demand for resources in LEDCs?
2. Describe two reasons why the increased demand for resources is putting pressure on people.
3. Discuss how the increased demand for resources is putting pressure on the environment.
4. Evaluate two benefits and two problems of one renewable energy source you have studied.

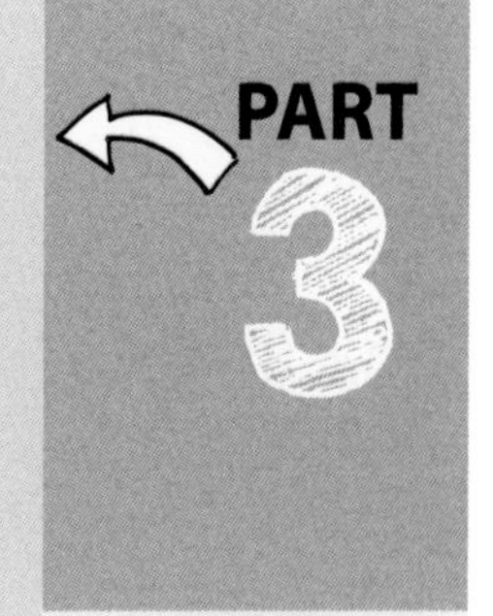

MANAGING WASTE TO PROTECT OUR ENVIRONMENT

Why has waste become such a major issue in the UK?

The Department of the Environment in Northern Ireland has noted that the amount of waste and the cost of dealing with this waste in Northern Ireland have been rising at a fast rate. There are three main issues that are affecting the management of waste in Northern Ireland:

1. **Shortage of landfill sites:** Over the last 50 years the main method of waste disposal has been landfill sites. However, Northern Ireland is running out of available sites for landfill. Pressure from the EU has also meant that local councils have been forced to move from a strategy based on landfill to one based on recycling.
2. **Environmental and health concerns:** The average household in Northern Ireland produces 1.29 tonnes of waste per year. With fewer landfills allowed, this means that treating and disposing of this material has become a problem.
3. **The need to meet government targets:** New EU legislation in 1999 emphasised the need for waste to be treated before being landfilled. New targets to reduce the amount of landfilled Biodegradeable Municipal Waste (BMW) were introduced.

Landfill site: This is a piece of land that is used for the dumping of rubbish. The site is usually an old quarry or area of reclaimed land.

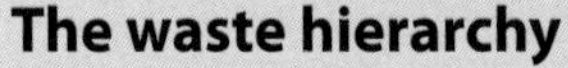

The waste hierarchy

The 'waste hierarchy' ranks waste management options in order of what is best for the environment. The best option is at the top of the pyramid and the least preferred option is at the bottom.

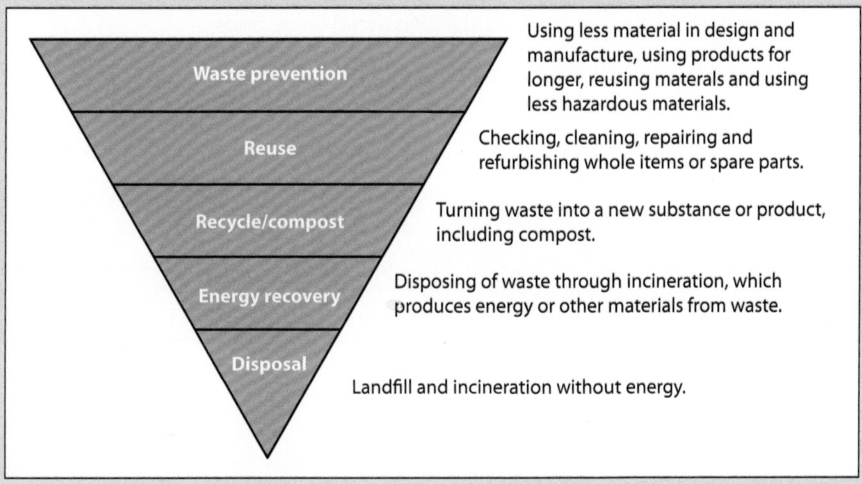

The waste hierarchy

Reduce, reuse and recycle

The waste hierarchy refers directly to the idea of 'reduce, reuse, recycle'. Through this, people are encouraged to engage in activities which will have an environmental impact.

Reduce: People are encouraged to buy less and to reduce the amount of energy that they actually use by turning lights off, taking shorter showers, reducing food waste and the amount of packaging they use, and sharing lifts to work and school.

Reuse: This is when materials are used again, without making them into new products. People are encouraged to use plastic food containers, refillable containers and reusable fabric shopping bags. Unwanted items can be sold online, at car boot sales or given away to charity shops.

Recycle: This is when waste materials are separated into component parts that can be incorporated into new products. Energy is used to change the physical properties of the material, turning them into an alternative final product. Upcycling is when waste materials are converted into items that are more expensive than the original article. Downcycling is when the waste materials are converted into items which are less expensive than the original article.

Why do we need a range of sustainable waste management approaches?

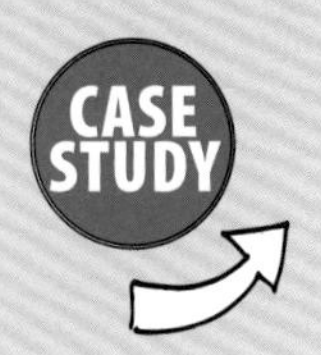

Case Study: Belfast City Council (a local government area)

Belfast City Council is the largest council in Northern Ireland and serves 270,000 people. The Council has joined with 10 other Councils to form arc21, which is one of three waste management groups in Northern Ireland.

Why does Belfast need a waste management strategy?

1. **Belfast produces a large amount of waste**
   The average house produces 1.29 tonnes of waste every year. In Belfast 130,000 tonnes of waste is sent to landfill every year. If this amount is not reduced in the future the Council will be forced to pay heavy fines.
2. **There is a shortage of landfill space**
   Existing landfill sites can only take a limited amount of waste and no new landfill sites are permitted.
3. **Environmental and health concerns**
   Many people who live near landfill sites are concerned about the smell and safety in the area, and want them closed.
4. **EU laws and targets**
   Belfast has not been able to meet current EU targets for waste management and further measures need to be taken if the Council is to avoid large fines.

What methods are being used to manage the waste?

1. **Recycling bins**
   Belfast City Council has invested money into supplying residents with a variety of bins:
   - **Black bin:** for general waste not suitable for recycling.
   - **Blue bin:** for items that can be recycled, eg paper, plastic bottles and cans.
   - **Purple recycling box:** for glass.
   - **Brown bin:** for items that are organic, eg grass cuttings, plants and leaves.
   - **Kerbside recycling box:** a black box that is collected by Bryson recycling for paper, cardboard, plastic bottles, textiles, tools and batteries.
   - **Food waste caddy:** for leftover food scraps.
   - **Home composter:** for garden waste.
2. **Reduction in black bin collections**
   Belfast currently recycles only 31% of its waste but this needs to increase to 60% by 2020 to meet EU targets. To address this, new recycling centres have been built across the city and black bin collections have been reduced from once a week to once every two weeks. This will encourage people to use their recycling bins more.
3. **Education and advertising**
   Belfast City Council has been involved in a comprehensive education and advertising campaign that has taken place over Northern Ireland in the last few years.
4. **Waste treatment facility**
   In June 2009, Belfast City Council gave arc21 permission to build a new waste treatment facility. The site will house a Mechanical Biological Treatment (MBT) facility, which will sort and compact waste before it is sent to landfill or an Energy from Waste (EfW) plant.

REVISION TIP

There have been a lot of recent developments in relation to waste management within the arc21 and Belfast City Council areas. Do an online search to keep up to date with the most recent decisions made about waste management in Belfast.

TEST YOUR REVISION

1. Explain one reason why waste has become such an important issue within Northern Ireland.
2. Why is there such a need for local councils to meet EU targets on waste management?
3. Describe how the waste hierarchy works.
4. Explain two methods that Belfast City Council is using to manage its waste.

SUSTAINABLE TOURISM TO PRESERVE THE ENVIRONMENT

The reasons why tourism has grown globally since the 1960s

"Tourism is the temporary, short term movement of people to destinations outside the places where they normally live and work, and activities during their stay at these destinations."

Since the 1960s there have been four key changes which increased the opportunity for travel:

1. **Increased leisure time:** The average worker spends 37 hours per week in work compared to 50 hours per week in the 1950s and also has more holiday entitlement.
2. **Increased disposable income:** Disposable income is the amount of money that households have left over when tax, housing and the basics of life have been paid out. People today have more money for short breaks, domestic holidays and overseas travel.
3. **Cheaper travel:**
   - *Increased car ownership:* Car ownership has increased from 2.3 million cars in 1950 to 24 million in 1999. With greater access to personal cars, people can explore different domestic and foreign tourist resorts.
   - *Increased use of aeroplanes for travel:* Following the Second World War there was a rapid advance in aircraft technology. Air travel became more affordable as the 'package holiday' was born.
   - *The rise of low cost air travel:* Until 2000, air travel was often the most expensive part of the holiday budget. Since then 'low cost airlines' have made flights more affordable.
4. **Increased health and wealth of pensioners:** Pensioners today are much wealthier than they used to be and modern medical care ensures that many of them are still active, fit and able to travel the world. As life expectancies have risen, tourists in the 'grey market' have around 20–25 years to spend time and money travelling the world.

Evaluate the positive and negative impacts of tourism

Tourism has become increasingly important to the economic development of a country and it has led to a number of positive and negative impacts.

IMPACTS OF TOURISM	POSITIVE IMPACTS	NEGATIVE IMPACTS
Cultural	• *Revitalisation:* When tourists come to an area, this triggers a revitalisation of neglected areas, government investment and the building of new community facilities. • *Rebirth of customs:* Tourism can cause a rebirth of local arts, craft and customs.	• *Inappropriate behaviour:* The behaviour of tourists can distort local customs and tourists can insult the culture, values and beliefs of the hosts. Crime and drunken behaviour might increase. • *Loss of local languages:* Local languages can be lost through under use.
Economic	• *Creates jobs:* The UNWTO estimates that 385 million people around the world are employed in the travel and tourism industry (11% of the total workforce). • *Foreign Currency:* Cash coming into a country can help it to develop and stabilise the economy. • *Improvements to infrastructure:* If a country attempts to improve its transport, utilities and communications to attract tourists, this will also benefit inhabitants.	• *Services:* The services in many resorts are designed and priced to cater for the tourist. Locals may have limited access to water services, entertainment and transport, and struggle to afford the inflated prices. • *Land and house prices:* Some tourists buy second homes which can increase the price of housing. Local people may not be able to afford the higher prices. • *Character changes:* Rural areas might lose their traditional characteristics. Traditional services and shops may be replaced with services that cater for the needs of the tourist.
Environmental	• *Sustainable tourism:* Visitors may actively participate in helping an area to be maintained and protected. • *Awareness:* Tourism to remote places can help expose the environmental problems and activities that are taking place there. • *Improvements:* The development of tourism can bring much needed improvements to derelict areas and tidy up clean waterways.	• *Soil erosion:* Erosion of soil, rock and vegetation can be caused by walkers and horse riders. This can damage fragile environments such as mountain areas. • *Congestion:* Too many people visiting areas at any one time can cause overcrowding and congestion, increasing carbon emissions. • *Pollution:* Tourists can pollute water, air and cause noise. This can also put pressure on water supplies.

Assess the impact of one sustainable tourism project on the local community and the environment

Ecotourism is described as tourism that:

- is environmentally sound.
- protects natural environments, wildlife and resources.
- is socially appropriate and respectful of local culture.
- does not damage local communities.
- provides economic benefits for local people.
- leads to sustainable tourism.

Green tourism (or sustainable tourism) is when tourism takes full account of its current and future economic, social and environmental impacts, addressing the needs of visitors, the industry, the environment and the host communities.

Case Study: Kenya (a LEDC case study)

Sustainable tourist resort: The Mara Intrepids Camp
Location: The savannah grasslands of the Maasai Mara National Reserve
Camp consists of: 30 luxury tents which are spread across a riverside

Kenya was one of the first African countries to embrace mass tourism. Most of the tourists here come from Europe and stay in coastal resorts but also spend some time on safari to an inland wildlife reserve. In 2009 Kenya earned over $887 million from tourism.

What makes this 'sustainable tourism'?
The Mara Intrepids Camp has received the second highest ecotourism award in Kenya – a silver award.

SOCIAL AND ECONOMIC IMPACTS

1. Jobs: Many of the staff at the camp are local Maasai people. This provides stable employment and a good income.

2. Staff training and opportunities: The camp gives professional training to all of its staff and first aid training is also provided.

3. Cultural visits: The camp organises a series of cultural visits for tourists which helps to build links with the local community.

4. Community Action: In June 2010 the hotel teamed up with MEAK (Medical and Educational Aid to Kenya) to set up a local 'Eye Mission to the Mara' where cataract operations and eye treatments helped many of the local people.

5. Supports education: The camp supports a local primary school in Talek and provides reading and writing materials.

ENVIRONMENTAL IMPACTS

1. Wildlife conservation: Guests are educated about wildlife conservation. Guides are trained not to disturb the animals whilst on safari drives and jeep numbers are kept to a minimum to reduce noise pollution.

2. Water: Grey water (from washing) and black water (from toilets) is filtered before being released.

3. Electricity: The majority of electricity is from a generator but char dust (compacted coffee husks) is used to heat water.

4. Waste: All kitchen waste is composted and other waste is recycled.

5. Food: The camp has an eco-garden where it grows its own vegetables.

6. Buildings: Many of the camp buildings are temporary and are designed to blend in with the local environment.

TEST YOUR REVISION

1. Explain why tourism has increased in the last 50 years. Give two reasons in your answer.
2. Evaluate the cultural impacts that tourism has had on an area.
3. State the meaning of 'ecotourism'.
4. Describe and explain some of the social and economic impacts that a sustainable tourism project could have with reference to a case study you have studied.

Getting the best grade possible

Every Mark Counts!

To get the best grade possible in your exam you need to understand how the course is structured and how the marks are allocated.

There are 3 units that you must complete to get your GCSE in Geography with CCEA:

- **Unit 1: Understanding Our Natural World** (Physical Geography)
  1 hour 30 mins exam paper (37.5% of the overall GCSE qualification)
- **Unit 2: Living in Our World** (Human Geography)
  1 hour 30 mins exam paper (37.5% of the overall GCSE qualification)
- **Unit 3: The Controlled Assessment/Fieldwork Report**
  (25% of the overall GCSE qualification)

There are two tiers of entry, Foundation and Higher Tier, and your teacher will usually decide which tier you enter.

So, how are you going to organise yourself to make sure that get the best grade possible? Let me give you a few simple pointers in the following areas:

1. Exam Paper Strategy
2. Exam Question Technique
3. Revision/Learning Strategy

PART 1

Exam Paper Strategy

You need to have a strategy to deal with your paper, to ensure you get it completed within the time given.

1. What to bring with you to the exam

You need to be properly prepared in a Geography exam, so bring a ruler, a pencil, a calculator, a protractor (angle measure) and a packet of five colouring pencils. I also think it's useful to bring a watch, so you have your own timekeeper on your desk to help you manage your time.

2. Just before the exam starts

The front of the exam paper is filled in and you are waiting to start … don't just sit and count down the seconds. Get your brain warmed up, thinking through the facts, figures and case studies you have learned. Before you know it you will hear…

3. 'You may begin'

Each of the two GCSE Geography examination papers is 1½ hours. There are 100 marks for each exam paper, plus 8 marks for spelling, punctuation and grammar. You will need to manage your time well to make sure you get the papers completed.

The tables below show how the two exam papers are structured, the marks for each question and how long you should spend on each question. Make sure that you work quickly through the shorter questions so that you have more time for the longer response questions.

Unit 1
Understanding Our Natural World

QUESTION	DESCRIPTION	MARKS (OUT OF 108)	EXAM TIMING (OUT OF 90 MINUTES)
Q1: Theme A: The Dynamic Landscape	One longer multi-part question dealing with rivers, coasts, flooding, river and coastal management (might also include map work).	50	45 minutes
Q2: Theme B: Our Changing Weather and Climate	One shorter question dealing with weather, anticyclones, depressions and climate change.	25	22½ minutes
Q3: The Restless Earth	One shorter question dealing with plate tectonics, volcanic features and earthquakes.	25	22½ minutes
Spelling, punctuation and the accurate use of grammar	An assessment will be made by the examiner in two questions on the paper as to how accurate your spelling, punctuation and use of grammar is through your answer.	8	Part of time allocation

Unit 2
Living in Our World

QUESTION	DESCRIPTION	MARKS (OUT OF 108)	EXAM TIMING (OUT OF 90 MINUTES)
Q1: Theme A: People and Where They Live	One longer multi-part question dealing with population, settlement and urbanisation (might also include map work).	50	45 minutes
Q2: Theme B: Contrasts in World Development	One shorter question dealing with the development gap, unequal development and solutions for improving development.	25	22½ minutes
Q3: Managing Our Resources	One shorter question dealing with the increased demand for resources, waste management and sustainable tourism.	25	22½ minutes
Spelling, punctuation and the accurate use of grammar	An assessment will be made by the examiner in two questions on the paper as to how accurate your spelling, punctuation and use of grammar is through your answer.	8	Part of time allocation

If you have time at the end

If you have time left, then it is important that you check through your answers and make sure that you have answered everything in as much detail as possible. Use every second to squeeze every last mark out of your paper that you can. There are no prizes for looking out a window at the end of an exam!

One little tip here is to use the handiest examination tool ever – your hand! Cover up your answers with your hand and ask yourself the question again. Think about what things you would expect in a good answer for this question and look under your hand to see how different you were! Add in anything you missed when writing your original answer.

Exam Question Technique

PART 2

It is important that you read each question thoroughly to make sure you know what you are being asked to do.

1. Circle the key words in the question

One of the biggest mistakes that candidates make is failing to answer the question written on the paper. You need to read every question **three** times. On the third reading it is a good idea to circle any command or key words. If you are asked to refer to a resource or a case study, make sure that you use specific facts and details that relate to the question.

2. Understand the command words in the question

Easy marks can be lost when students don't answer the question in the right way. There is a big difference between an answer that asks you to **describe** a graph and one that asks you to **explain** the reasons why the graph is a particular shape. Make sure that you know what the most common command words actually mean.

Compare	What are the main differences and similarities?
Contrast	What are the main differences?
Define	State the meaning (definition) of the term.
Describe	Use details to show the shape or pattern of a resource, or give details of a known case study or concept. What does it look like? What are the highs, lows and averages?
Discuss	This often means that you must describe and explain. You should argue a particular point but you might have to address both sides of an argument (agree and disagree).
Explain	Give reasons why a pattern or feature exists using geographical knowledge.
Evaluate	Look at the positive and negative points of a particular strategy or theory and give an overall concluding statement.
Identify	Choose or select.

3. Think about the structure of the question

Sometimes the longer exam questions can prove tricky. If they seem wordy, try breaking down the question into chunks. This will help you to structure the answer fully.

For example, the 2012 Unit 1: Understanding Our Natural World (Higher Tier) exam paper, Question 1 (g) (ii) asked the following question for 7 marks.

> *"Evaluate **two** river management strategies used on a river that you have studied outside the British Isles."* (© CCEA 2015)

To answer this question:

- You must first realise that this is referring to a) river management and b) outside the British Isles (eg the Yangtze River, China).
- You should **evaluate** two management strategies, which means a) briefly describe two management strategies within the context of the river and b) look at the positive and negative features of this particular strategy.

In some cases the marker will be looking to give 1 mark for selecting an appropriate case study. The two river management strategies will each get 3 marks and there is a lot to do for 3 marks in each case. You must also provide an overall concluding statement, which clearly shows whether each strategy was mostly positive or mostly negative.

4. **Use the marks as a guide**

Remember to use the marks allocated alongside each question to help you to:

a) manage your time in the exam.

b) work out how much depth you need to go into for an answer.

- For a question worth 7 marks you should be aiming to spend around 7 minutes. Don't spend any longer on it or you won't get the paper finished in time. The examiner will concentrate on your answer, so don't write the question out again, get straight to the point and avoid waffling.
- The number of marks available for each question dictates the number of lines provided for each answer. Make sure you use all the line space given for each answer.

5. **Practice your case studies/model answers**

During your GCSE course, you will look in depth at a lot of case studies. You will read a lot of contextual information that you won't be asked about in an examination but you need to understand for the case study to make sense. Make sure that you learn **only what you need to know** for each case study. Learn the location, the key facts and the main points that are raised about what the case is trying to prove (or disprove).

Practice questions involving case studies as much as you can. They make up a sizeable chunk of the questions in your examination paper. You should take a look at the pattern of 'longer questions' that get asked for case studies and practice preparing and writing model answers to these questions.

PART 3

Revision/Learning Strategy

"WE ARE SUCCESSFUL BECAUSE WE PRACTICE WHAT WE ARE NOT GOOD AT."

(Richie McCaw, New Zealand All Blacks Rugby team captain)

The secret ingredient to successful revision is that you must LEARN your topics. Revision can be boring and it can be difficult to stay focused. However, you have to train your brain to learn things in the depth that you need. The following are some useful tips that can help you:

1. Start your revision early and plan it carefully so that you have enough time to cover the whole subject at least three times before the exam season starts.
2. Revision is not just reading; it involves taking notes and processing information.
3. You can't do that much revision sitting at your computer. New technologies provide lots of amazing new ways to support your revision but try not to become distracted by the games, the drawings and the timetables. You may need to turn off your computer, tablet or phone, or leave your devices in another room while you get down to the hard work of learning the facts and figures.
4. How much revision you need to do is a very individual thing. Some people like to revise in short bursts (eg 50 minutes), with mini breaks (eg 10 minutes) in between to have a cup of coffee, check their text messages or go for a walk. Others like to revise for longer periods and set themselves a target (eg 3 hours), which they aim to meet, followed by a reward such as watching a TV programme. It doesn't matter how you organise yourself – all that matters is that you put the time and effort in.
5. Remember, just because you are sitting at the desk in your bedroom doesn't mean that you are actually achieving anything. Don't fool yourself; if you don't get the work done, you won't get the marks you want. Be honest and if you are struggling to focus, ask your friends and parents to check on you more often to keep you on task.

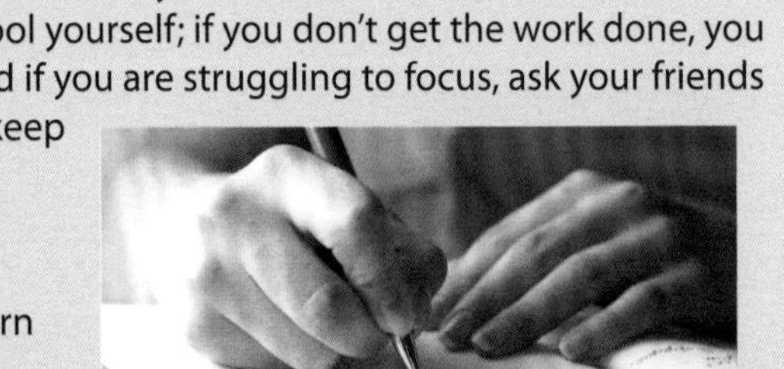

Understanding the way that YOU learn is very important. It is unlikely that you will be able to learn and remember things in the same way that your friends do. Therefore, it can be useful to practice a variety of revision and learning techniques so that you can find the one that works best for you.

Revision and learning techniques

There are many different revision and learning techniques but let me suggest some that have worked for my students in the past:

1. Condense 3

This is a very traditional technique that works well if you find it difficult to remember things over a long period of time. It does take a lot of time and effort but the aim is to create a set of 'trigger' words which will help to prompt knowledge in the middle of the exam.

Step 1: Go through a particular topic and make notes about what you need to remember.

Step 2: Now go through the notes you have made and try to condense these a second time onto an A5 page (one side).

Step 3: Condense the information for a third time by taking note of the key words on your A5 page and writing them on one A3 page. Your aim is to have one big page for each major topic and this will be packed with the key 'trigger' words that you need to remember.

Step 4: Sit and learn the trigger words. Take each word in turn and say it aloud. Put your finger on the word on the page and think about what other information this trigger word leads you to.

2. Mind maps

This technique allows you to see the 'big picture' and is great for organising information. It can also be very useful when trying to work out how to answer a question. Using the example below as a template, draw your own mind map for each topic and use them to answer practice questions.

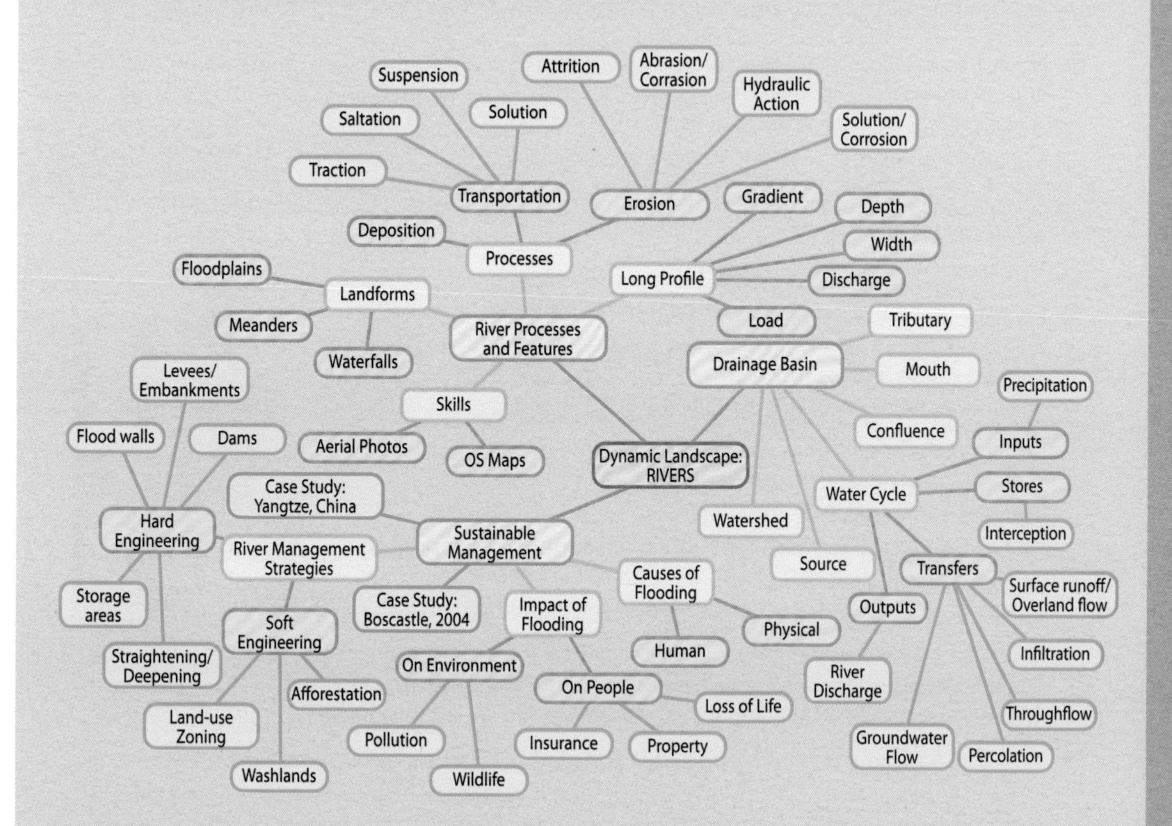

3. Traffic lighting

This technique offers a simple way for you to identify:

- what you already know (green).
- what you nearly know (yellow).
- what you do not know (red).

You can use highlighters or coloured dots as you go through your notes to indicate how well you know and understand various parts of the course.

4. Card sort

You might find that you learn more by making your own revision information cards. There are a number of ways you could do this:

- Make one card for each topic or case study. Pack the card with information and key facts that will help support an answer. You could even have advantages on one side and disadvantages on the other.
- You could create your own Geography 'Top Trumps' type game, where you have key facts and features on a card and you have to remember where the case study place is.

5. Make your own podcast

Finally, there are some very good podcasts available that may help your revision but why don't you make your own? There is a lot of free software online that allows you to record your own MP3, so you can sit on the bus or go to bed listening to the facts and figures from your Geography course.

Some advice for parents/carers

Parents/carers, it's all too easy to put too much pressure on our teenagers. We might think that they do not realise how important these exams are but my experience is that most teenagers know precisely how much rests on their performance. It's hard to revise for up to 10 different subjects over a 4 month period but how you support your teenager can make all the difference. Here are some suggestions on how you can help your teenager through the exam season:

1. Try not to nag your teenager about the lack of revision that they seem to be doing. If you feel you need to push your son or daughter to more work, do this positively. Try asking questions such as 'What did you learn about tonight?' rather than 'How much did you do tonight?'
2. Offer your help with organising files, asking questions, getting pens and paper, and recording your teenager's favourite TV programmes so they can watch them when they're finished their revision for the day.
3. Create a quiet and supportive atmosphere, as proper learning is most effective in silence. You can help here by turning the TV down and providing a 'quiet place' where your teenager can work. This will also allow them to get used to the silence of the exam hall.
4. Pop in from time to time with a cup of coffee or their favourite snack, or just sit on the bed for a quick chat. This is called a 'positive intervention' and you might be surprised how motivating it can be when teenagers feel supported! Your teen will be more likely to keep working and the treat will give them more energy and the incentive to do a little more.
5. Everyone needs study breaks. Current research shows that teenagers should have breaks every 45 minutes or so. You can help to manage these but again keep it positive, such as 'Do you want me to make you a cup of tea for next break? When will that be?'
6. Take care – more and more young people today are starting to burn out because of exam stress. Keep an eye on how they're coping and if you are concerned that they are working too hard, have a chat with their teachers or your GP. Sometimes the best thing you can do is take them out for some pizza or order them out to the cinema with their mates!

Exam Question Practice

About this section

The following pages provide a practice exam paper, containing exam style questions and examples of student answers in *blue*. These student answers provide a basis for your own response and will be followed by some examiner tips in *red* to show how the answers could have been improved.

The majority of the questions in the book are aimed at both the foundation and higher tiers – though some questions are reserved only for higher tier. You will see an icon alongside each question to indicate whether it is foundation tier (F), higher tier **(H)** or both (F) **(H)**.

Unit 1
Understanding Our Natural World

QUESTION 1
THEME A: THE DYNAMIC LANDSCAPE

1 (a) Study **Fig 1** which shows a drainage basin. Answer the questions which follow.

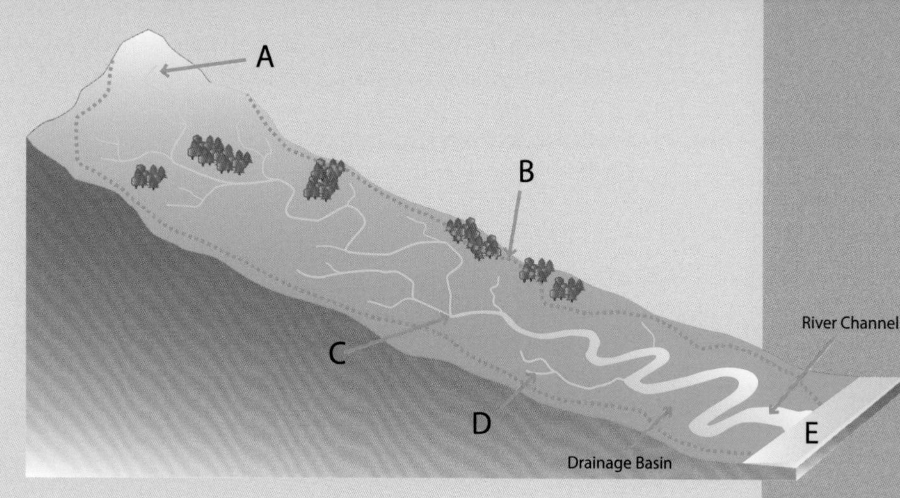

Fig 1

Key	
A =	Where the river begins
B =	The area of high ground which separates one drainage basin from its neighbour
C =	The place where two rivers join
D =	A small, narrow river that will join with the main river
E =	Where the river meets the sea

(i) Complete the key for **Fig 1** by labelling features A–E. [5]

F **H**

Key	
A = *source*	Where the river begins
B = *watershed*	The area of high ground which separates one drainage basin from its neighbour
C = *confluence*	The place where two rivers join
D = *tributary*	A small, narrow river that will join with the main river
E = *mouth*	Where the river meets the sea

5/5 marks awarded

This is a very straightforward question. The candidate should be able to identify and label the parts of the drainage basin system easily. Each answer has been correctly identified. 1 mark for each correct answer.

H

(ii) Name **two** transfers of water within the drainage basin system. [2]

1. groundwater
2. infiltration

1/2 marks awarded

The mark scheme for this question notes that there is 1 mark for correctly identifying the transfers as surface runoff/overland flow, infiltration, throughflow, percolation and groundwater flow. Groundwater is NOT correct as the answer needed to have 'flow' to show a movement through the system.

FH

(iii) State the meaning of the term **groundwater flow.** [2]

Groundwater flow is when water travels downwards into the soil. If the soil has infiltrated too much water it becomes saturated.

1/2 marks awarded

The candidate has described the term infiltration rather than groundwater flow. The answer needs to have some reference to water moving down and back towards the river. For example, a simple definition might be 'water moves slowly through the soil and the rocks back into the sea'.

(b) Study **Fig 2** which shows how load size varies along the course of the Glenarm River in Co Antrim. Answer the questions which follow.

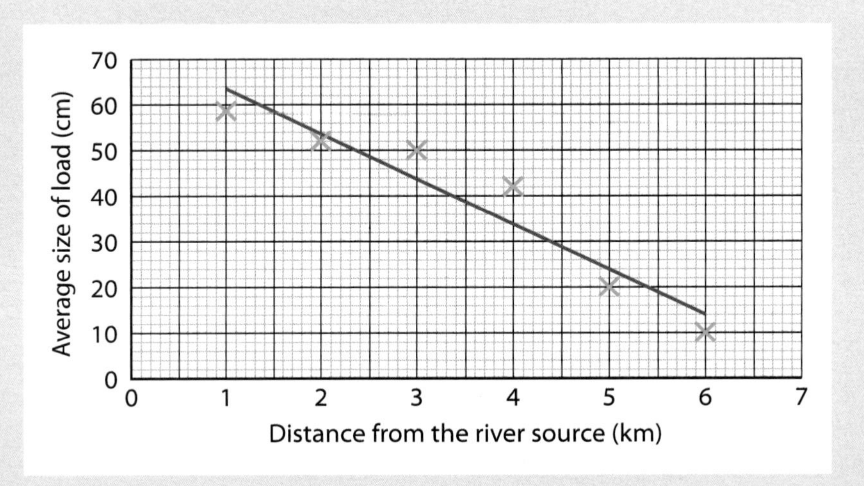

Fig 2

H

(i) Describe how load size changes along the Glenarm River. [4]

When the load is closer to the source it is larger (cm). The size of the load at 1 km is 58 cm. As the load travels further down stream it becomes smaller in size. At 4 km from the river source the load is 42 cm and as it travels to 6 km the size is 10 cm.

3/4 marks awarded

Longer questions are marked using levels of response:

Level 1 = 1 mark

A simple, correct statement regarding the graph or bed load change in general.

Level 2 = 2–3 marks

A correct statement and elaboration that relates to the graph. For 2 marks the answer must contain at least one figure on size and for 3 marks there must be at least two figures on size.

Level 3 = 4 marks
A correct statement regarding trend, referring to at least two figures on size and recognising that from 4 km the load size reduces faster than before.

The mark scheme for this question notes that this answer gets 3 marks based on the comments on stone size. However, this answer will not be awarded 4 marks as there is no mention of the sudden drop in stone size at 5 km and 6 km.

FH

(ii) Underline the **two** types of erosion below which might help to explain the variation shown in **Fig 2**.

Saltation **Abrasion** **Traction** **Attrition** **Suspension** [2]

2/2 marks awarded
The candidate has correctly identified Abrasion and Attrition as the processes that are involved in shaping the rock in a river. The other three words are all transportation processes within the river.

H

(c) Name **one** transportation process that might be active in a river and explain how it carries material downstream. [3]

Saltation is a transportation process that happens when some bits of rock in the river are bounced along.

2/3 marks awarded
The mark scheme for this question notes that there is 1 mark available for accurately naming one transportation process and another 2 marks are available for a valid response that explains the process.

This answer accurately names saltation (the alternatives are: traction, suspension and solution) but the explanation is quite basic and needs a bit more depth. A better answer might explain that this process only occurs when heavier particles cannot be held up in the flow of the river all of the time, or that the stones are bounced along the river bed.

FH

(d) With reference to a river in the British Isles, explain the physical and human causes of a flood. [8]

Name of river: Valency

Causes of the flood:

Physical – It had rained 12 out of 14 days that month. The day of the flood it had rained 185 mm in 5 hours and this meant that the soil was saturated. Since the soil could no longer infiltrate, the water ran down the surface of the drainage basin.

Human – The bridge's arch was very low so as the fast river flowed underneath, debris (eg trees) got trapped below the arch. This created a large blockage which caused all of the surrounding land to get flooded with water.

6/8 marks awarded
The mark scheme for this question notes that if the candidate names a river outside the British Isles or does not name a river, a maximum of Level 1 will be awarded.

Level 1 = 1–2 marks
A river within the British Isles is correctly named. Causes of river flooding are stated briefly.

Level 2 = 3–6 marks
Causes of flooding are described with some explanation but there are no specific facts and figures linked to a river in the British Isles. A maximum of 4 marks if only physical or human factors are used.

Level 3 = 7–8 marks
The causes of flooding are described in detail with a full explanation. Answer should include two facts relating to the river within the British Isles.

In this answer the candidate has attempted to give facts to support the case study but still lacks some detail. For example, the date (16 August) could be stated and the amount of rainfall was actually between 200 mm and 300 mm. However, there is some solid geographical explanation and the candidate has done well to balance both the physical and human factors within the answer.

H

(e) Coastlines are constantly shaped by waves. State **two** facts about constructive waves. [2]

Constructive waves have a strong wash and a weak backwash.
Constructive waves build up the beach as it brings sediment up the beach.

2/2 marks awarded
The mark scheme for this question notes that there is 1 mark for each correct fact related to constructive waves. The candidate here has identified two separate facts, so maximum marks can be awarded.

F H

(f) Study **Fig 3** which shows a photograph of a coastal spit at Spurn head in Yorkshire. Answer the questions which follow.

University Of Cambridge Collection Of Air Photographs/Science Photo Library

Fig 3

Identify the two features labelled **X** and **Y.** Choose your answers from the list below.

Salt marsh **Deposited sand and shingle** **Longshore drift** **Prevailing wind** [2]

X = Salt marsh
Y = Longshore drift

1/2 marks awarded
The mark scheme for this question notes that there is 1 mark for correctly identifying each of the two features. X is salt marsh and Y is the location of the deposited sand and shingle. Here the candidate has answered the first question correctly but the second answer is incorrect.

FH

(g) Explain the formation of a spit. [6]

Eroded material from the coast is transported by longshore drift. Prevailing winds cause the waves to change direction. The eroded material is transported by longshore drift and is now deposited where the coastline changes direction, which allows the spit to form as constant deposition occurs. Prevailing winds cause the spit to hook and the water behind this spit becomes still and turns into marsh land. Spits take hundreds of years to form.

3/6 marks awarded

The mark scheme for this question notes:

Level 1 = 1–2 marks
The answer makes reference to the movement of sand.

Level 2 = 3–4 marks
Reference is made to either the conditions required for a spit to develop or the process involved.

Level 3 = 5–6 marks
Explanation is made for both the conditions required for a spit to develop and the processes involved.

In this case the candidate has attempted to write about both the processes and conditions but does not include enough detail to support the answer. There is not enough depth for this to be a Level 3 answer. A Level 2 answer was allocated but the processes were not fully developed and a mark in the lower part of the level was awarded. It is important that candidates clearly understand and can explain a sequence of events in relation to spit formation.

(h) **(i)** Explain the formation of a stack. [6]

H

At any cliff-face where the sea and land meet, cracks can start to develop in any weakness found in the rocks. These cracks are usually caused by attrition as the sea attacks the rock on a regular basis. The cracks will eventually form into caves. The erosion will continue in the cave (mostly through abrasion) and the cave might be eroded enough to form an arch. Waves will continue to erode and the weight of the rock in the arch will become too heavy and the roof of the arch will collapse to form a stack.

6/6 marks awarded

The mark scheme for this question notes:

Level 1 = 1–2 marks
A simple, correct statement about stack formation.

Level 2 = 3–4 marks
A partial explanation relating to stack formation.

Level 3 = 5–6 marks
A full explanation of how stacks are formed, noting the process of erosion and the development of the features from crack, cave, arch to stack.

This answer deals with the question well. There is some discussion of the role that erosion plays in the process and a clear understanding of the steps leading up to the development of a stack.

H

(ii) With reference to a case study from the British Isles, evaluate the sustainability of a coastal management strategy you have studied. [8]

Spelling, punctuation and accurate use of grammar. [4]

Newcastle (Co Down): Sea Wall

Newcastle had a storm which ruined their initial sea wall. The sea wall that can be seen today reflects and absorbs some of the wave energy. It has a deep foundation that prevents erosion on the sea bed. The sea wall protects shops, tourist attractions and residential homes. It cost at least £10 million. It is a large concrete wall that surrounds the entire coast of Newcastle. Some people say it is an eyesore and some say it has ruined the natural beauty of the area. Although, it needs constant maintenance in order to make it effective.

5/8 marks awarded

The mark scheme for this question notes:

Level 1 = 1–2 marks

A simple description or evaluation of coastal management which may not name a location.

Level 2 = 3–5 marks

The coastal management strategy is evaluated but there is a lack of detail.

Level 3 = 6–8 marks

The sustainability of one coastal management strategy is evaluated and the answer will include two facts/figures/places relating to the named coastal area. Some judgement or conclusion is needed for full evaluation.

This answer does contain some good detail in relation to sea walls at Newcastle but needs to go further. There is a need for balance in the positive and negative aspects of how sustainable this strategy actually is. The candidate also needs to include some form of final statement about the sustainability of this particular approach (and maybe compare it to other strategies which could have been used).

Spelling, punctuation and accurate use of grammar

3/4 marks awarded

There are 4 marks available for spelling, punctuation and grammar in this question.

Threshold performance = 1 mark

Candidates spell, punctuate and use the rules of grammar with reasonable accuracy in the context of the demands of the question.

Intermediate performance = 2/3 marks

Candidates spell, punctuate and use the rules of grammar with considerable accuracy. They use a good range of specialist terms.

High performance = 4 marks

Candidates spell, punctuate and use the rules of grammar with consistent accuracy and effective control of meaning in the context of the demands of the question. They use a wide range of specialist terms with precision.

In this case the candidate achieved 3 out of the 4 possible marks. Use of punctuation could be improved and the answer would have benefitted from a greater use of specialist terms.

QUESTION 2
THEME B: OUR CHANGING WEATHER AND CLIMATE

2 (a) Study **Fig 4** which shows a weather forecast for an anticyclone over Northern Ireland in July. Answer the questions which follow.

A. The temperature will be a very warm 28 °C.
B. The wind speed will be calm.
C. Warm air will come from a south-easterly direction.
D. There will be no rain.

Fig 4

Weather element	Instrument
A	
B	
C	
D	

Table 1

F H

(i) Using **Fig 4** complete **Table 1** by writing in the names of the instruments that could be used to collect information on each of the weather elements in the forecast. [4]

Weather element	Instrument
A	Thermometer
B	Anemometer
C	Wind vane
D	Rain gauge

4/4 marks awarded
The candidate has successfully identified each of the 4 pieces of equipment that are used to measure the elements of the weather. There are no marks for identifying the weather element.

F H

(ii) State the name of the air mass that is most likely to have brought this weather. [1]

Tropical maritime

0/1 marks awarded
The most likely airmass to bring this type of weather is Tropical Continental, as this brings warm and dry weather.

H

(iii) Explain why there will be no rain. [3]

Anticyclones rarely bring rain as they are high pressure. Also tropical maritime air mass doesn't bring a lot of rain, maybe even none as it is coming from the south-east. Also, the air mass will be going over France so it won't pick up any water on the way.

1/3 marks awarded:
The mark scheme for this question notes:

Award 1 mark
For an answer that has a simple statement.

Award 2 marks
For an answer that has a simple statement with a consequence.

Award 3 marks
For an answer that has a statement, consequence and elaboration. For example, there are few clouds in the sky as the area experiences high pressure and is sinking. As the air sinks it will become warmer. This means that condensation does not happen and clouds cannot develop.

This candidate has continued to discuss the tropical maritime air mass from the question before but manages to get commentary of some value in the last sentence. More elaboration is needed to increase marks in this question.

H

(b) Weather forecasts are created by the Met Office in the UK. They use satellite images to help build a forecast. Answer the question which follows.

Name the type of satellite which passes around the earth from pole to pole. [1]

Polar orbiting

1/1 mark awarded
The candidate has correctly identified this type of satellite. An alternative answer is polar.

(c) Study **Fig 5** which shows where greenhouse gas emissions originated from in the USA in 2010. Answer the questions which follow.

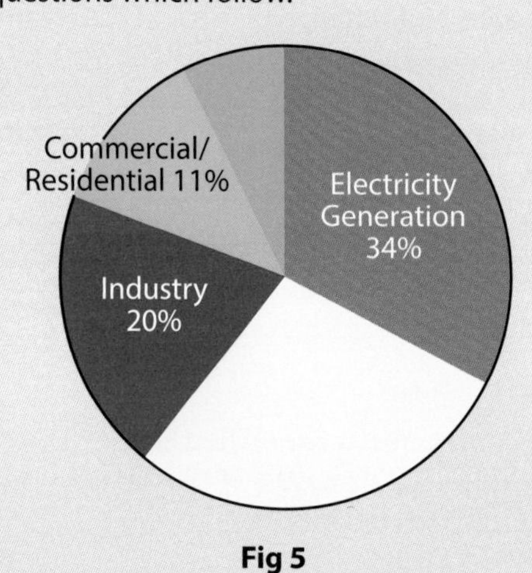

Fig 5

FH

(i) Complete **Fig 5** by inserting the correct labels on the pie chart using the information below.

Agriculture = 7%

Transportation = 27% [2]

2/2 marks awarded
The candidate has correctly identified the correct areas and has labelled them appropriately. Only 1 mark can be awarded if the candidate fails to also include the actual percentage number in the answer.

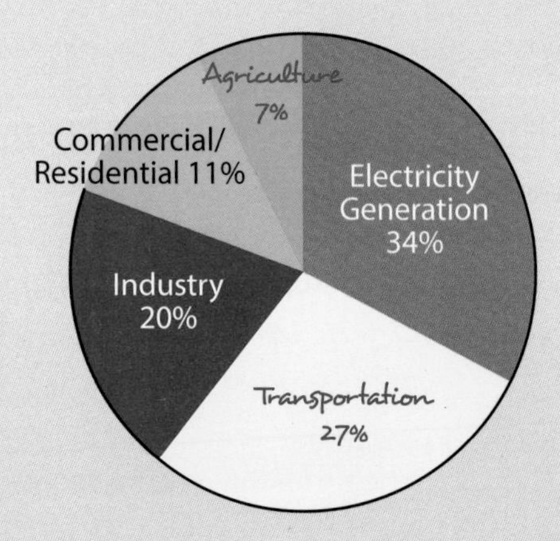

FH

(ii) With reference to a named country that you have studied, describe the likely effects of climate change on the environment of a named country. [6]

Spelling, punctuation and accurate use of grammar. [4]

Britain: Climate change will affect the environment in lots of different ways. The first thing is that the warmer temperatures will cause the sea levels to rise as icebergs are melting. This means that some areas will become flooded and people will not be able to live close to the sea anymore. The economy might also do better as people will buy more ice creams in the summer and farmers will be able to grow more crops as it will be a lot warmer.

4/6 marks awarded

The mark scheme for this question notes:

Level 1 = 1–2 marks

An answer that provides a limited factual account of effects related to the environment. An answer that does not refer to a named country will be limited to this level.

Level 2 = 3–4 marks

An answer that describes two separate factors but one might be more detailed than the other.

Level 3 = 5–6 marks

An answer that describes two separate factors in some depth and has included valid case study material with at least two facts/figures and places.

In this case the candidate has correctly identified and explained one environmental factor but the second factor strays into an economic effect rather than environmental. To be considered for Level 3 the answer would also need to include more specific details in relation to places. For example, what places might be flooded or what plants will be affected by the climate change.

Spelling, punctuation and grammar

3/4 marks awarded

There are 4 marks available for spelling, punctuation and grammar in this question. For a full explanation of the breakdown of spelling, punctuation and grammar marks, refer to Question 1 (h) (i).

In this case the candidate achieved 3 out of the 4 possible marks. The use of punctuation could be improved and the answer would have benefitted from a greater use of specialist terms.

(d) Study **Fig 6** which is a graph showing some of the targets for changes in greenhouse gas emissions by 2012 agreed at the Kyoto conference in 1997. Answer the questions which follow.

Fig 6

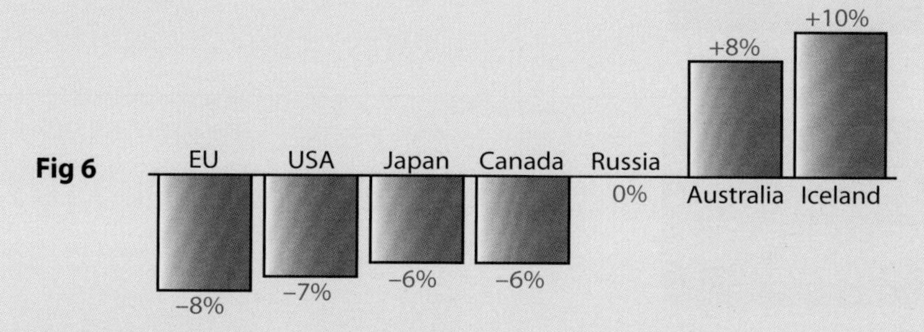

(i) Using **Fig 6** state the name of the area that had the biggest target for reducing greenhouse gas emissions by 2012. [1]

FH

The EU

1/1 mark awarded

The EU were collectively trying to reduce greenhouse emissions by 8%.

FH

(ii) Briefly outline **two** methods which can be used to cut down the use of private cars to help deal with climate change. [4]

One method of cutting down the number of cars on the road is to make sure that public transport is good. In cities like London money has been spent to improve buses and trains so that people will travel in these rather than their cars. Another way is to charge any cars when they come into the city.

3/4 marks awarded

The mark scheme notes that candidates should discuss:

Investing in public transport; congestion charging or car sharing. Candidates should refer to two separate methods. If only one challenge is mentioned a maximum of 2 marks is to be awarded. There are 2 marks for each method.

In this case, the answer refers to two methods. The candidate explains the use of public transport well but only mentions the second method in a basic way and needs to go into more depth.

QUESTION 3
THEME C: THE RESTLESS EARTH

3 (a) Study **Fig 7** which shows some types of rock. Answer the questions which follow.

Name of rock	Rock type
Granite	
Limestone	
Slate	**Metamorphic**

Fig 7

FH

(i) Complete **Fig 7** by identifying the rock type of each rock. One has been completed for you. [2]

Name of rock	Rock type
Granite	Igneous
Limestone	Sedimentary
Slate	**Metamorphic**

2/2 marks awarded

The candidate has correctly identified the two additional rock types. 1 mark for each correct answer.

(ii) Explain how basalt is formed. [3]

Basalt is formed due to a volcano. The volcano erupts and lava spreads over the land. Basalt cools fairly quickly on the surface and this means it has little evidence of a crystalline structure.

3/3 marks awarded

The mark scheme for this question notes:

Award 1 mark

For an answer that has a simple statement.

Award 2 marks

For an answer that has a simple statement with a consequence referring to lava cooling on the surface.

Award 3 marks

For an answer that has a statement, consequence and elaboration which refers to cooling and small crystals forming. For example, a volcano erupts and the molten magma rises and flows onto the surface, where it starts to cool quickly and forms small crystals that will harden into basalt.

The candidate in this case has provided a good answer which explains and elaborates the formation of basalt from a volcano and maximum marks can be awarded.

H

(b) Study **Fig 8** which shows part of the earth's structure. Answer the questions which follow.

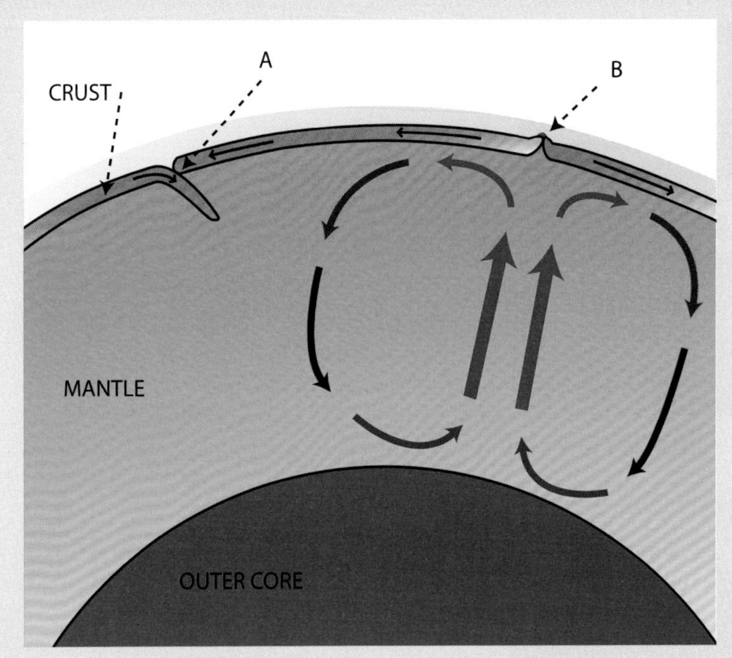

Fig 8

FH

(i) Name the features **A and B**.

A ____________________

B ____________________ [2]

A Crust
B Volcano

1/2 marks awarded

The answer to A is either ocean trench or subduction zone. The answer to B is mid-ocean trench, volcano or ridge.

In this case the candidate has answered the first answer incorrectly but the second is correct.

FH

(ii) Use **Fig 8** to help you to explain why plates move. [3]

Convection currents move in the mantle, as extreme heat from the earth's core heats the rock in the mantle, this rock becomes less dense and causes it to rise to the surface and come back down as it cools. This then causes the plates to move.

2/3 marks awarded

The mark scheme for this question notes:

Award 1 mark

For an answer that has a simple statement.

Award 2 marks

For an answer that has a simple statement with a consequence referring to convection currents.

Award 3 marks

For an answer that has a statement, consequence and elaboration which refers to plates being moved.

In this case the candidate has made a good attempt to answer the question but needs to go into more detail. More precision is needed in the explanation to ensure that maximum marks are achieved.

(iii) Complete **Fig 9** by drawing in arrows to show the direction of the plate movement. Also mark the likely place where most earthquakes would originate with an X. [3]

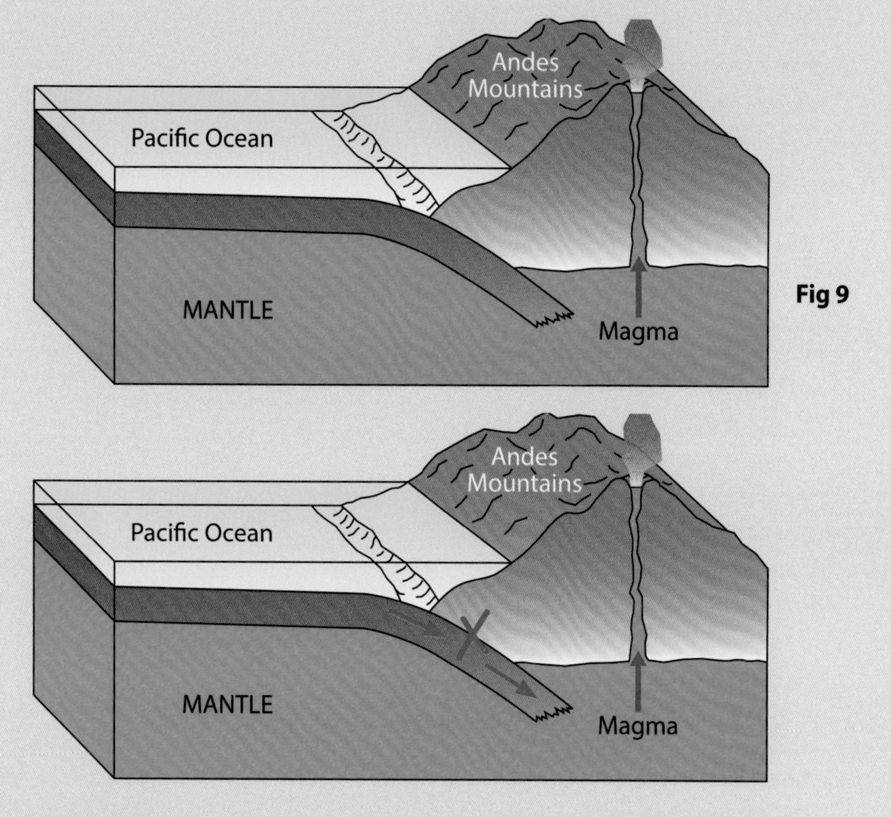

Fig 9

3/3 marks awarded

See above diagram for a copy of the correct answers. The candidate has put the arrows in the correct place and has identified that earthquakes can take place within the subduction zone where the two plates meet.

FH

(iv) Name this type of plate boundary. [1]

Destructive plate boundary

1/1 mark awarded

The correct plate boundary was identified as the destructive plate margin. Another acceptable answer is converging.

FH

(c) Liquefaction is one physical effect which can take place following an earthquake. Answer the questions which follow.

(i) State the meaning of the term **liquefaction.** [2]

Liquefaction is when an earthquake causes buildings to sink into the ground.

1/2 marks awarded

Award 1 mark

For a basic statement.

Award 2 marks

For a full definition that refers to earthquakes as the cause.
For example, liquefaction occurs when an earthquake hits an area and shakes the wet soil. The shaking causes the water within the soil to start to rise to the surface, and this process turns solid soil and rock into a liquid mud.

In this case the answer is purely a basic statement and requires a bit more elaboration as to how liquefaction takes place to get the second mark.

FH

(ii) Explain the causes behind an earthquake that happened in a **LEDC** that you have studied. [3]

Name of LEDC: Haiti

The Caribbean plate is moving past the North American plate. This causes a lot of friction and a strike-slip movement occurs. This is a conservative plate boundary.

2/3 marks awarded

The mark scheme for this question notes:

Award 1 mark

For an answer that has a simple statement referring to plate movement. A maximum of 1 mark is awarded if there is no named earthquake or the earthquake is located in a MEDC.

Award 2 marks

For an answer that has a simple statement with a consequence referring to how plates move and the friction or stress that is built up.

Award 3 marks

For an answer that has a statement, consequence and elaboration which refers to how plates move and friction or stress was built up to create an earthquake. There must be at least one fact that relates to the named earthquake.

The candidate has given some good facts and depth about the plates and the type of movement. For maximum marks the answer also needs to explain how the movement here brought about the release of pressure that led to an earthquake. Sometimes it is easy to give a complicated answer but forget the simple statement that explains what is happening to start an earthquake.

H

(d) With reference to an earthquake in a **MEDC** that you have studied, evaluate the immediate and long term strategies that were implemented after the event. [6]

Name of MEDC: Japan

The Great Tohoku earthquake took place in Japan on 11th March 2011 at 248 pm. The earthquake caused many different problems for the people of Japan. It created over 300,000 refugees and people found it difficult to get even the most basic things like food, water and shelter. The weather was very cold and people struggled with the weather and climate. Another impact was that new tsunami barriers had to be built which would stretch 19 m high as the tsunami waves had been much bigger than expected.

4/6 marks awarded

The mark scheme for this question notes:

Level 1 = 1–2 marks

An answer that provides a simple statement of at least two immediate and long term strategies.

Level 2 = 3–4 marks

An answer that describes two separate immediate and long term strategies in some depth that fit within the parameters of the case study.

Level 3 = 5–6 marks

An answer that describes two separate immediate and long term strategies with a full discussion that evaluates what was good and what was not good.

This candidate has managed to develop some good depth in relation to two valid immediate and long term strategies that were used during the Japanese *earthquake. However, the answer needs to go into a little more depth and also evaluate the response more. What was successful? What did not work? What aspect of the response could have been further improved? It is this aspect of evaluation that keeps the answer limited to a high Level 2.*

Unit 2
Living in Our World

QUESTION 1
THEME A: PEOPLE AND WHERE THEY LIVE

FH

1 (a) Study the Ordnance Survey extract of Belfast (1:50,000 scale) in **Fig 1**. Answer the questions which follow.

Fig 1

FH

(i) State the straight line distance from the Car Park at Belfast Zoological Gardens at GR 325811 to the Car Park at the Odyssey arena at GR 348747. [2]

6 km

0/2 marks awarded

The correct answer is 6.75 km. No marks are awarded. An answer between 6.65–6.85 km will be awarded 2 marks with answers 6.55–6.64 km or 6.86–6.95 km receiving 1 mark.

FH

(ii) Part of Belfast's CBD is located in grid square 3374. State **two** pieces of map evidence which support this statement. [2]

There are a lot of car parks in this area that shows that many people might drive into this area to go to work or to go shopping. Many of the roads bring traffic into the city and meet close to the CBD.

2/2 marks awarded

The candidate has correctly identified two pieces of evidence. The high number of church buildings or a discussion of the convergence of communications (road, rail, motorways) are both acceptable answers.

FH

(iii) Describe **one** way in which the area in grid square 3574 is typical of an inner city area. [2]

Many of the streets in this area are long and straight in a grid like pattern which probably means that the streets are terraced houses which have been built close to factories.

2/2 marks awarded

Award 1 mark

For a basic valid description making reference to the straight streets, long rows of buildings or a high density of buildings.

Award 2 marks

For a more developed description, for example, the buildings are terraced houses or this is an area just outside the area of the CBD.

H

(b) Study **Fig 2** which shows a photograph of the Titanic Quarter development in inner city Belfast (GR 350749). This area has recently been developed with new residential properties. Answer the question which follows.

Source: Chris Bennett

Fig 2

H

Many newcomers have moved into the Titanic Quarter Arc development in the last few years. Using only information from the Ordnance Survey map and the photograph explain why this inner city area has attracted newcomers. [6]

The inner city area has attracted many newcomers to the area as recent property development has taken place in the new Titanic Quarter. The creation of new apartments has attracted more people into the inner city area. The photograph shows that the apartments have been built very close to the old industrial area, as you can see a H&W (Harland and Wolff shipyard) crane in the background. The map shows that this area has been built close the industrial area of Queens Island which means that this is regeneration.

4/6 marks awarded

Levels of response are used in this question:

Level 1 = 1–2 marks

A basic answer might refer to the map or photo evidence.

- The area is close to the CBD and amenities
- It is close to major road and railway connections
- It is part of a regeneration area

Level 2 = 3–4 marks

An answer that uses evidence from both the map and the photo but lacks detail.

Level 3 = 5–6 marks

An answer that goes into some depth about why the area might be attractive to newcomers. It must use both map and photo evidence.

This answer contains some useful depth and has attempted to use both the map and the photo. To achieve a Level 3 the candidate would need to go into further depth, such as the area is developing jobs, education and other services, which will encourage more people to live there, within close access of the CBD. This must be supported with specific evidence from the photo and the map.

(c) **Fig 3** shows an aerial photograph of part of The Titanic Quarter site and the Belfast Harbour area which is located in grid squares 3575 and 3676. Answer the questions which follow.

Fig 3

Image courtesy of Titanic Quarter Limited

(i) Using **map** evidence outline **two** reasons why this is a good location for an industrial zone. [4]

There are good transport links with wide roads, making this area good for an industrial zone as it allows the transport of heavy and large industrial machinery to and from the area. It also contains buildings that are large enough to house factories and enable industrialisation.

H

3/4 marks awarded

An answer will usually focus on the proximity of a good communication network or space for development. The area is close to motorway and primary routes/railway stations/Belfast port/Belfast City Airport. There is also much room for expansion.

Award 1–2 marks

For two basic statements or one statement with a consequence.

- Good communications
- Room to expand
- Near a large city

Award 3–4 marks

For two valid statements with consequence that mention specific evidence from the map or one well developed statement.

This answer raises some good points that address the question but requires more evidence from the photo and the map.

H

(ii) State the direction of the Odyssey area (GR 348749) from Belfast Castle (GR 327 792). [1]

South West

1/1 mark awarded

The correct answer is South West.

H

(d) **(i)** Urbanisation has been a significant process taking place throughout the 20th and early 21st centuries. It is defined as being an increase in the percentage of people living in cities. Explain **two** causes of urbanisation referring to both MEDCs and LEDCs in your answer. [6]

Urbanisation is the growth of urban areas as people move in from rural areas and the size of the place swells. Many people moved into cities like Belfast and Glasgow in the early 20th century because there were opportunities to earn a good living in big factories and industries like shipbuilding. Since then many people have started to move out of the city and have returned to live in the countryside. This is called counter urbanisation.

3/6 marks awarded

Level 1 = 1/2 marks

Mentions either one cause or two causes but in very little detail.

Level 2 = 3/4 marks

An answer that includes two causes but these might not be fully developed or address both LEDCS and MEDCs.

Level 3 = 5/6 marks

An answer that refers to the causes of urbanisation in both LEDCs and MEDCs and clearly addresses two separate and distinct causes of urbanisation.

In this answer, the candidate has started to address the question and has some good information about one cause of urbanisation in a MEDC. However, there is no mention of a second cause or information related to urbanisation in a LEDC. This answer shows a candidate who has perhaps not read the question properly and needs to mention both MEDCs and LEDCs for a Level 3 answer.

H

(ii) In many MEDCs there has been an opposite movement of people away from the large urban areas. State the name of this process. [1]

Counter urbanisation

1/1 mark awarded

Award 1 mark

For counter urbanisation or urban to rural migration.

H

(e) Describe and explain some of the characteristics of a shanty town you have studied. [6]

Shanty town is the name given to the spontaneous housing in Sao Paulo, a LEDC in Brazil. The people who live in a shanty town like Paraisopolis find it really difficult to get formal jobs. There is a lot of unemployment in the city and people are forced to work in the informal sector or turn to crime – they might shine shoes or work as drug dealers. Houses in the area are temporary and basic, and will lack basic services like electricity, drinking water and sewage. Over a million people live here and there is a big difference between people who are rich and poor.

5/6 marks awarded.

Level 1 = 1/2 marks

A short answer that describes some basic characteristics in general terms.

Level 2 = 3/4 marks
An answer that either describes both characteristics of the shanty town with some elaboration but still lacks specific facts or only explains one of the characteristics in some depth.

Level 3 = 5/6 marks
An answer that both describes and explains the two characteristics identified (employment and housing) with specific detail added, including at least 2 facts/figures for a maximum mark of 6.

This answer dealt comprehensively with the question. There is good description and explanation of some of the characteristics that would be expected within a shanty town. However, the answer would benefit from explaining why people find it difficult to get formal jobs and further discussion about the pressure caused by large numbers of people arriving into the city.

FH

(f) Study **Fig 4** which shows population pyramids for Germany and Turkey in 2010. Answer the question which follows.

Describe **two** differences between the population pyramids of Germany and Turkey. [6]

Fig 4

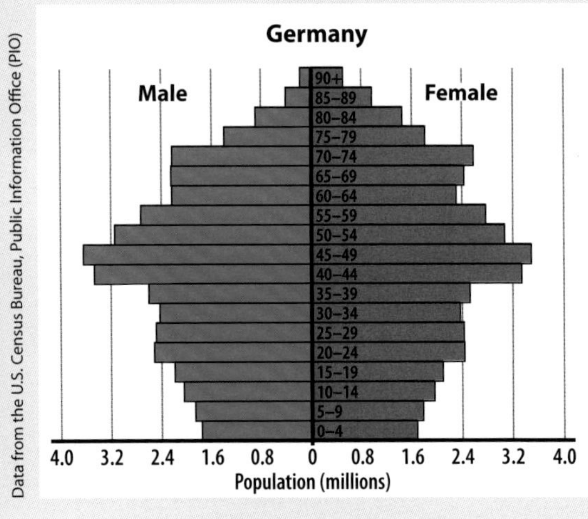

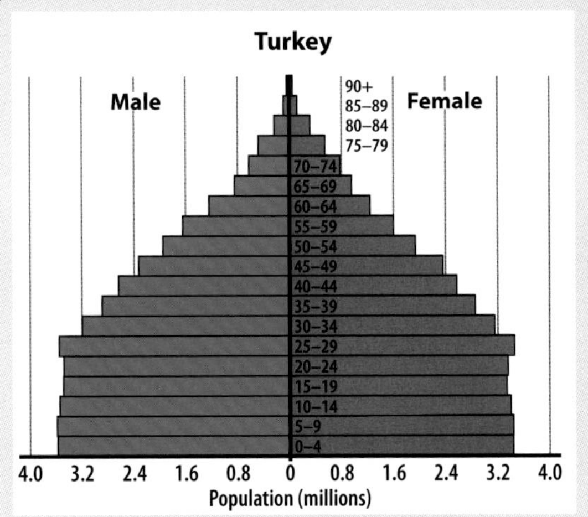

Data from the U.S. Census Bureau, Public Information Office (PIO)

The bottom of Turkey's pyramid is much wider than Germany's. This is because Turkey has a larger birth rate (7 million people aged 0-4) than Germany (3.2 million people aged 0-4). The top of Turkey's pyramid (3 million people aged 75+) is much narrower than Germany's (over 6 million aged 75+). This is because Turkey also has a much higher death rate than Germany. Therefore, Turkey shows characteristics of a youthful population while Germany shows characteristics of an aged population.

6/6 marks awarded

Award 1 mark
For an answer that has a valid statement.

Award 2 marks
For a valid statement relating to both Germany and Turkey. For example, there are more young people in Turkey than in Germany and there are more people aged over 75 in Germany than in Turkey.

Award 3 marks
For a valid statement with elaboration and clear reference to the pyramids, such as the shape of the pyramid or the bars. For example:

- There are proportionally more people from the age of 40 upwards in Germany than in Turkey.
- There are fewer young people in all age groups up to the age of 34 in Germany. One of the largest cohorts for Turkey is for those aged 0–4 (where around 7 million children are found) this compares to only around 3.2 million German children.

There are 3 marks for each of the TWO descriptions.

This candidate has put together a very good answer. One part of the answer compares the birth rates and the description is supported through the use of accurate figures and a reference to the shape of the pyramid. The second description deals with death rate and again is supported with appropriate facts and figures.

(g) Study **Fig 5** which is a graph showing the world's population growth from 1700 to the present. Answer the questions which follow.

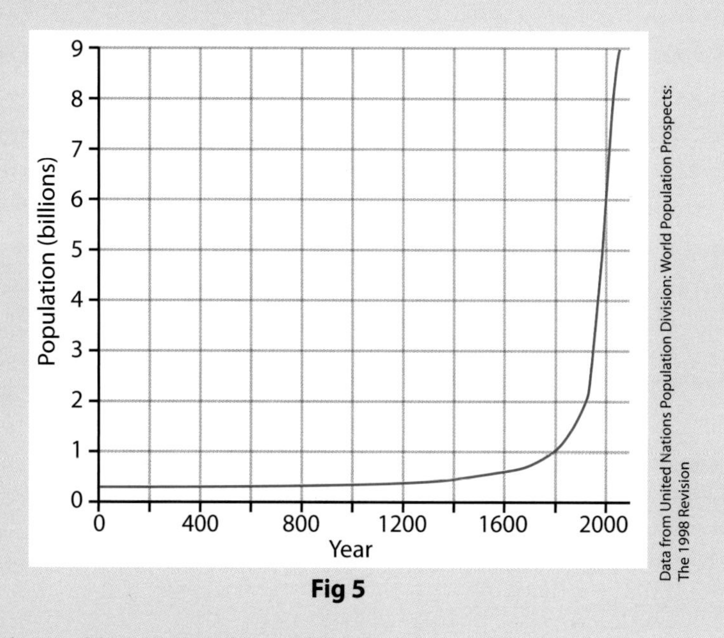

Data from United Nations Population Division: World Population Prospects: The 1998 Revision

Fig 5

FH

(i) State the world's population in 1800. [1]

1 billion

1/1 mark awarded
There is one mark for correctly identifying 1 billion people.

FH

(ii) State the year when the world's population reached 5 billion people. [1]

2000

1/1 mark awarded
There is one mark for correctly identifying the year 2000.

FH

(iii) Explain fully why the world's population increased rapidly from the year 1900. Give two reasons in your answer. [4]

Over the last 100 years the population of the world has been growing at a very fast rate. The reason for this is that in poor countries (called LEDCs) they do not have access to contraception. Also, in some societies it is more acceptable to have lots of wives and men with lots of children are seen as being more powerful than men with no children.

2/4 marks awarded
Level 1 = 1/2 marks
An answer that explains one reason in full or that looks at two reasons in basic detail and lacks elaboration.

Level 2 = 3/4 marks
An answer that fully explains two reasons in some depth with full elaboration. There are many different arguments which are acceptable when answering this question but candidates must talk about the reasons for the global population explosion. They might

argue that birth rates are high (especially in LEDCs) and that death rates have been on the decrease (initially in MEDCs but more recently in LEDCs as well).

This answer includes a well argued explanation for high birth rates in LEDCs but has not gone on to discuss a second reason for the population increase.

H

(h) **Evaluate the positive and negative impacts of international migration for one named country within the European Union which you have studied. [8]**

Spelling, punctuation and accurate use of grammar. [4]

The migration of people from Turkey to Germany had both positive and negative impacts on Germany. The positive impacts are: after World War 2 the male workforce of Germany was seriously low due to the losses during the war. The migration of gastarbeiters (guestworkers) helped to improve the German economy. The working conditions in Germany were the best in Europe and the amount of young workers meant that the birth rate in the country would continue to be high. Negative impacts were that the workers came over and stayed a lot longer than expected. The Germans did not want to give them citizenship. The increase in ethnic diversity lead to a wave of racial violence, as many Germans were concerned that Turks had taken their jobs.

4/8 marks awarded

The mark scheme for this question notes:

Level 1 = 1/2 marks

A simple, unbalanced answer, looking at only positive or negative impacts in a basic way.

Level 2 = 3–5 marks

An answer that looks at both the positive and negative impacts but lacks specific case study material or does not evaluate the impacts.

Level 3 = 6–8 marks

A well balanced answer that will include more than one positive impact and more than one negative impact. It will include two or more specific facts or figures and an evaluation, which must include a concluding statement explaining whether this migration is mostly positive or negative.

This answer contains some good detail but it fails to achieve a Level 3. There are some positive and negative impacts noted in relation to Germany but these could have used further elaboration. The candidate has spent too much time explaining the history of the case study, which would have been better used for evaluating these impacts and how they made a difference in Germany.

Examiner comment (spelling, punctuation and grammar)

4/4 marks awarded

There are 4 marks available for spelling, punctuation and grammar in this question.

Threshold performance = 1 mark

Candidates spell, punctuate and use the rules of grammar with reasonable accuracy in the context of the demands of the question.

Intermediate performance = 2/3 marks

Candidates spell, punctuate and use the rules of grammar with considerable accuracy. They use a good range of specialist terms.

High performance = 4 marks

Candidates spell, punctuate and use the rules of grammar with consistent accuracy and effective control of meaning in the context of the demands of the question. They use a wide range of specialist terms with precision.

In this case the candidate achieved 4 out of the 4 possible marks.

QUESTION 2
THEME B: CONTRASTS IN WORLD DEVELOPMENT

2 (a) Study **Table 1** which shows two indicators of development for five countries. Answer the questions which follow.

Table 1

Country	Life Expectancy (years)	GNI Per capita ($)
Norway	81	47,557
Iceland	82	29,354
Zimbabwe	51	376
Mali	51	1,123
Congo (DR)	48	280

Figures from: 2011 Human Development Report, United Nations Development Programme.

(i) Using information from the table, identify ONE country that might be considered a MEDC and ONE country that might be considered as being a LEDC. [2]

F H

MEDC: Norway

LEDC: Zimbabwe

2/2 marks awarded

The candidate has correctly identified Norway as a MEDC. The other possibility was Iceland. The candidate has also identified Zimbabwe correctly as a LEDC. The other possibilities were Mali or Congo (DR).

The Human Development Index (HDI) often uses information such as Life Expectancy and GNI to help indicate development.

(ii) Name one other indicator which is also included when calculating the Human Development Index (HDI) for a country. [1]

F H

Years of schooling

1/1 mark awarded

The modern HDI index uses mean years of schooling (in years) and expected years of schooling (in years) within its matrix. However, literacy rates is also an acceptable answer.

(iii) Explain why the HDI is one of the most effective indicators of development. [4]

F H

The Human Development Index is effective because it is a combination of social indicators such as literacy rate, birth rate and years of schooling as well as the economic indicator of gross national product. This combination gives the statistic which shows a balance of the social and economic progress of the country, leading to excellent levels of accuracy. This is why it is the most effective indicator of development as it looks at both sides of the story and doesn't depend too much on one or the other.

4/4 marks awarded

The mark scheme for this question notes:

Level 1 = 1 mark

An answer that gives a simple statement of what the HDI is.

Level 2 = 2/3 marks
A statement that shows some understanding of what is involved in the HDI – that it is a composite measure including social and economic data.

Level 3 = 4 marks
A statement that shows an understanding of what is involved in the discussion of HDI with some further description of how the social and economic indicators are needed to measure the development.

In this answer the candidate notes that birth rate is involved which is not the case (it is life expectancy). Otherwise the answer is strong and goes into some depth about the different indicators and why these are effective, so it is awarded full marks.

(b) Study **Fig 6** which shows the amount of Fairtrade coffee sales in the UK. Answer the questions which follow.

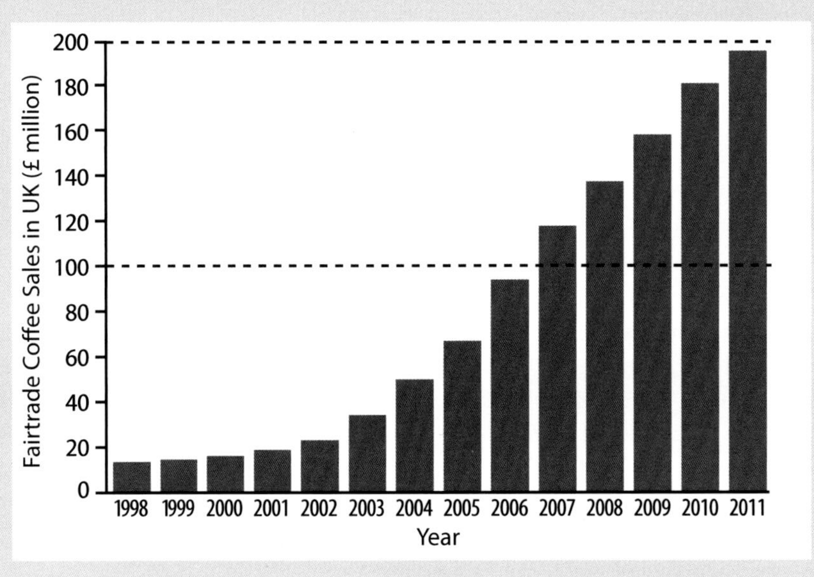

Fig 6

F H

(i) Identify the year when Fairtrade coffee sales were at their peak. [1]

2011

1/1 mark awarded
There is one mark for identifying 2011 as the correct year.

F H

(ii) State one problem linked to the trade in coffee that might arise for a LEDC. [2]

Countries have introduced tariffs to try and protect their own industries. This often means that LEDCs have to sell the raw material to a country rather than selling processed goods which would generate more money for the LEDC

2/2 marks awarded
Some of the things that can provide trade issues for LEDCs in the sale of coffee might include a reliance on primary products, tariffs and the impact of Trading Blocs. Candidates can discuss any valid issue here.

In this case the candidate has identified a valid issue and has gone on to elaborate in some depth the impact that the trade might have. In this case, the coffee will often be exported before processing (roasting). This process will be carried out in the MEDC so that they can continue to make more money out of the trade.

(iii) State the meaning of the term **Fairtrade.** [2]

FH

This is when the LEDC receives a salary of at least minimum wage from the MEDC which it trades with. This means the LEDC producer receives a sustainable salary where the size of the farm land does not matter and minimum wage is higher than the local wage.

1/2 marks awarded

Award 1 mark

For a basic definition.

Award 2 marks

For a more detailed definition. For example, Fairtrade is a strategy used to improve trading conditions in LEDCs and help farmers get paid a fair price for their products. It cuts out the middle men in the trading system, meaning more money goes to the producer and allows them to use extra income to protect the environment.

In this answer the candidate mixed up the terminology in relation to minimum wage and has not addressed the issue of why this is fair in enough depth.

(iv) Describe and explain how Fairtrade is a sustainable solution that deals with problems of unequal development. You should refer to places in your answer. [5]

FH

Fairtrade is a sustainable solution as it allows the people of the LEDCs such as Kenya to receive a fair salary. This provides the farmers with a sustainable income and the farmer and the local community can come together to co-operate and develop a reasonable payment level. This also improves relations and breaks down trade barriers, allowing the LEDC to economically develop and receive a fair amount of money for their primary production.

4/5 marks awarded

Level 1 = 1 mark

A basic answer that attempts to explain Fairtrade. The answer may lack reference to places or sustainability.

Level 2 = 2–3 marks

An answer that explains how Fairtrade is helping a country to develop. One place should be referenced for a Level 2 answer.

Level 3 = 4–5 marks

An answer that addresses all the parts of the question (Fairtrade, sustainability and a reference to two places).

In this case the candidate has put forward a strong argument but needs to go further to discuss an additional place and how this might be a sustainable solution.

(c) State the meaning of the term **aid.** [2]

FH

Aid is when one country or organisation gives help or resources to another country. This might be water, doctors or tents and might be short term aid when there is an emergency like an earthquake or long term aid over a period of years.

2/2 marks awarded

Award 1 mark

For a basic definition.

Award 2 marks

For a more detailed definition.

In this case the candidate has put together a comprehensive description of what aid is and how it works. They have clearly explained the different aspects of aid and gone into enough detail to achieve full marks.

H

(d) Evaluate the economic and social improvements that have come about due to a sustainable project that uses appropriate technology in a LEDC that you have studied. [6]

Spelling, punctuation and accurate use of grammar. [4]

A sustainable project that uses appropriate technology which we have studied was the development of wells and hand pumps with the charity Fields of Life in Uganda. Fields of life have been building wells to provide safe, clean drinking water for local people. This brings economic improvements because it means that the children and women do not have to walk 12 miles each day to fetch water from the local river. This saves a lot of time, which means that children can go to school and women can start to work and earn money. Also, some of the women have been able to use the water to make bread and snacks for local tourists. This is bringing more money into the local community. There have also been social improvements, which mean that the community can work together more.

4/6 marks awarded

The mark scheme for this question notes:

Level 1 = 1–2 marks

A basic statement that introduces a sustainable project with limited discussion of the improvements which have been brought about.

Level 2 = 3–4 marks

An answer that focuses on only one of the improvements or has not gone into enough depth across both of the improvements listed in the question.

Level 3 = 5–6 marks

An answer that covers all aspects of the question, with relevant facts and details to support the answer. It discusses the economic and social improvements that the project has brought and evaluates the impact of the project on the local people.

In this answer the candidate has provided some very strong case study material and the discussion of the economic improvements and the evaluation is done well. However, the answer is not balanced and there is little discussion or evaluation of the second improvement – therefore the answer cannot achieve a Level 3 mark and is restricted to a high Level 2.

Examiner comment (spelling, punctuation and grammar)
4/4 marks awarded

There are 4 marks available for spelling, punctuation and grammar in this question.

Threshold performance = 1 mark

Candidates spell, punctuate and use the rules of grammar with reasonable accuracy in the context of the demands of the question.

Intermediate performance = 2–3 marks

Candidates spell, punctuate and use the rules of grammar with considerable accuracy. They use a good range of specialist terms.

High performance = 4 marks

Candidates spell, punctuate and use the rules of grammar with consistent accuracy and effective control of meaning in the context of the demands of the question. They use a wide range of specialist terms with precision.

In this case the candidate achieved 4 out of the 4 possible marks.

Questions 2 (a) (i), (b) (i), (ii), (c), (d) author's own in exam style

QUESTION 3
THEME C: MANAGING OUR RESOURCES

H

3 (a) Study **Fig 7** which shows the amount of carbon dioxide emissions per capita across the United Kingdom. Answer the questions that follow.

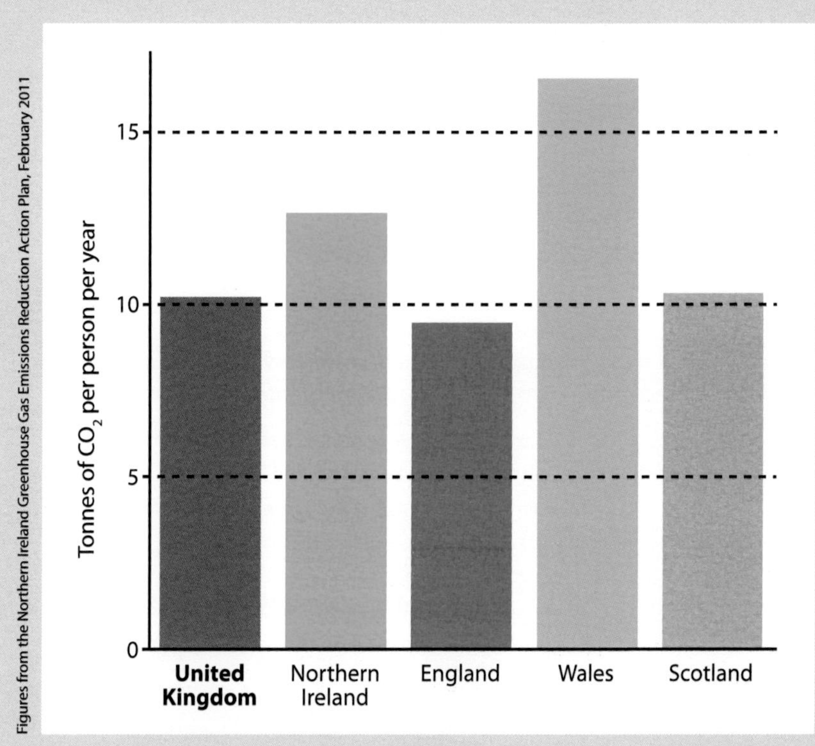

Fig 7

H

(i) Describe the pattern of carbon dioxide emissions per capita across the United Kingdom shown in **Fig 7**. [4]

In the UK the amount of carbon dioxide emissions per person per year is just over 10 tonnes. The only area of the UK where the amount of emissions is below this is England (around 9 tonnes) but the other 3 regions are higher. Scotland is just over 10 tonnes and Northern Ireland and Wales are much higher than that.

3/4 marks awarded

Award 1 mark
A simple statement with no figures quoted.

Award 2–3 marks
An accurate statement that makes reference to each of the regions on the graph and uses figures to back up the statement of description.

Award 4 marks
Accurate statements that refer to all 5 of the areas on the graph with figures and a statement of comparison for each.

In this case the candidate has started well, identified some of the regions and made a comparison with the UK. However, more facts and figures would be needed for the final two regions (Wales and Northern Ireland) to achieve 4 marks.

FH

(ii) Describe **one** sustainable way of managing waste which has been used by a local government area that you have studied. [3]

The arc 21 programme used EfW (energy from waste) which uses the food waste produced from homes and turns this into compost. This compost is then used as a source of heating for 30,000 homes in the area providing a sustainable way to manage waste.

2/3 marks awarded

Answer must relate to an appropriate named local government area such as Belfast City Council.

Award 1 mark
For a simple statement of the sustainable method.

Award 2 marks
For a simple statement with a consequence.

Award 3 marks
For a statement with a consequence plus elaboration which includes factual information related to the named local government area.

In this case the candidate has accurately described one sustainable way of managing waste but they have not grounded the case within the 'area that was studied'. To achieve full marks the candidate would also need to include the name of the local government.

H

(b) With reference to a case study of a city within the EU, identify and evaluate two measures that were used to manage traffic in a sustainable manner. [4]

In the city of Freiburg in Germany a number of measures were taken to manage the traffic problems in the city.

1. Public transport: The city council in Freiburg has invested a lot of money in an integrated transport network across the city. The main part of this is a large electric tram network. These trams are efficient, quick and cheap. There are also some special 'bendy buses'. Energy for these comes from renewable sources, however, some people think that the transport is not as good at off-peak times.

2. Cycling encouraged: Over 400 miles of cycle track have been developed and many people will cycle around the city. Car use is discouraged and taxes are high for using cars. The downside of this is that it can be difficult to get shopping and big purchases back home.

4/4 marks awarded

Award 1 mark
For a simple statement that identifies and discusses one named strategy.

Award 2 marks
For a statement that identifies a sustainable strategy and evaluates it fully.

This should be repeated for the second strategy (2 x 2 marks).

In this case the candidate has identified and clearly evaluated two separate sustainable measures with some useful reference to the case study city.

FH

(c) Suggest **two** ways in which the environment in tourist destinations might be negatively impacted by any increase in visitor numbers. [4]

1. This could reduce the area of land available for wildlife as there is an increased desire for hotels and shopping construction to meet the tourists' needs.

2. This could increase the carbon footprint in the environment of the tourist destination as there are more tourists arriving and departing plus travelling by car, jeep, bus and plane, which increases the carbon dioxide released into the atmosphere.

3/4 marks awarded

Award 1 mark

For a simple statement.

Award 2 marks

For a statement with some explanation of how the impact occurs.

This should be repeated for the second statement (2 x 2 marks).

In this case the candidate has obtained 2/2 marks for the first impact but the explanation for the second impact is not as strong and needs more development to justify full marks.

(d) **(i)** State the meaning of the term **ecotourism**. [2] FH

Ecotourism is when people travel to a country without causing damage to the environment as they do so and measures are put into place to protect the environment, wildlife and resources.

2/2 marks awarded

Award 1 mark

For a basic definition.

Award 2 marks

For a more detailed definition.

In this case the candidate has put together a comprehensive description of what ecotourism is. They have clearly explained the different aspects of ecotourism and have a good command of the question so full marks can be awarded.

(ii) Evaluate the impacts of tourism on the culture and economy of tourist destinations. You should refer to named places in your answer. [8] FH

The culture and economy are greatly impacted by tourism in tourist destinations such as Kenya. This is a location which attracts high levels of tourism. This can affect the economy positively as in 2010, 190,000 jobs were created by tourism which helped the local economy and made $887 million in 2010. However, 30% of these jobs were seasonal, so they can be unreliable as they do not provide income all year. Also, most of the money made from the tourists goes back to the international company and is not invested in the local community. There are positive cultural impacts as well - tourists can find out more about the way that the Kenyan people used to live and this will increase their respect for the local culture, while providing entertainment for the tourist. However, it can lead to attacks on the tourists as they bring their rich belongings and might encourage robberies and kidnaps. Also, sometimes displaying the culture makes people feel like performers rather than sharing an important lesson from history.

6/8 marks awarded

The mark scheme clearly notes that in order to reach Level 3 the answer must evaluate at least one positive and one negative impact, refer to both cultural and economic impacts and must refer to named places. There are no marks for discussing environmental impacts.

Level 1 = 1–2 marks
The answer will contain some relevant information but might miss out on either positives or negatives or only discuss one impact.

Level 2 = 3–5 marks
The answer will outline both cultural and economic impacts with some evaluation of positive or negative impacts.

Level 3 = 6–8 marks
The answer has made specific reference to at least one place and has developed both positives and negatives for both the economic and the cultural impacts. There is a fair amount of detail in the answer and the candidate is in command of the question.

In this case, the candidate has shown a good level of knowledge in relation to Kenya. However, the answer could have been a little more specific, especially in relation to the discussion of cultural impacts. A little deeper evaluation required here to achieve a higher Level 3 mark.

Questions 3 (b) & (d) author's own in exam style

Copyright Information

Picture credits

Author: 8 (bottom, both), 20 (bottom), 40 (right), 92 (all), 93 (all)

Chris Bennett: 101

Francisco Antunes (licensed under the Creative Commons Attribution-Share Alike 2.0 Generic license, http://creativecommons.org/licenses/by-sa/2.0/deed.en): 58

iStockPhoto: 79, 82

Met Office (licensed under the Open Government Licence v1.0): base data for 25 (bottom)

Neighbourhood Statistics (NISRA) (map based upon Crown Copyright and is reproduced with the permission of Land & Property Services under delegated authority from the Controller of Her Majesty's Stationery Office, Crown copyright and database right 2015 PMLPA No 100496): 49

Ordnance Survey of Northern Ireland (based upon Crown Copyright and is reproduced with the permission of Land & Property Services under delegated authority from the Controller of Her Majesty's Stationery Office, Crown copyright and database right 2015 PMLPA No 100496): 11 (bottom), 100

SSE and Dong Energy: 74

Titanic Quarter Limited: 59, 102

University of Cambridge Collection of Air Photographs/Science Photo Library: 88

U.S. Army Corps of Engineers photo by Ann Cameron Siegal: 20 (middle)